BUILDING THE SOCIALLY RESPONSIBLE EMPLOYMENT POLICY IN THE BALTIC STATES

Published by
Baltic Sea Academy e.V.
Dr Max Hogefoster
Blankeneser Landstrasse 7,
22587 Hamburg, Germany

Editorial Correspondence: editor@baltic-sea-academy.eu

All papers in this publication are scientifikally reviewed by Prof. habil. dr. Aleksandras Vytautas Rutkauskas, Vilnius Gediminas Technical University end Ph.D. of Social science Algimantas Misiūnas.

Printed by:
BoD-Books on Demand, Norderstedt, Germany

ISBN 9783735790484

Part-financed by the European Union (European Development Fund and European Neighbourhood and Partnership Instrument) within the QUICK IGA project. This publication does not necessarily reflect the opinion of the European Commission.

We are very grateful to the European Commission for the financial support and also to the Joint Technical Secretariat of the INTERREG IVB Programme for the support and advice.

Content

Foreword

The project "Innovative SMEs by Gender and Age (QUICK-IGA)" addresses the following objectives:

✓ levelling of equal opportunities for women south of the Baltic Sea with the ones of northern countries;

✓ strengthening the promotion of innovation in small and medium-sized enterprises by developing working cultures that explicitly improve the equal opportunities of women;

✓ supporting regional development in order to optimally develop human capital and competitiveness through gender and education policy.

On four levels the project focuses on the following activities:

1. Individuals: boosting motivation and work ability, thus increasing the rate of women participating in working life, through the training and education of consultants and the development of a manual;

2. Enterprises: fostering working conditions that meet women's needs and personnel development through the transfer of best practice, qualifications and coaching.

3. Organisations: competences and commitment of 45 chambers and 15 universities to supporting innovation and equal opportunities.

4. Policy: developing a strategy programme, five regional/national agreements and two action programmes to promote equal opportunities and innovation in SMEs.

The outputs and results of the project were published in the Baltic Sea Academy series for the following activities:

Data and principles

Two investigations were carried out for the countries and regions of the Baltic Sea region as the consistent basis for all further work:

a) demographic and economic analysis in the BSR countries and regions;

b) analysis of regional education and labour markets.

The results of these investigations were published in spring 2013 as part of the Baltic Sea Academy series under the title "Economic Perspectives, Qualification and Labour Market Integration of Women in the Baltic Sea Region".

Education

The results of the analysis have been incorporated into two new education products:

a) concept and curriculum for a train the trainer programme for the permanent implementation of training courses for consultants by universities and academies;

b) concept and curricula for a training and coaching programme for consultants to enhance their advisory competences on improving work structures in SMEs in order to increase the labour participation of women and older people, as well as innovation capacities.

Both training courses have been trialled multiple times in various locations and scientifically evaluated. The curricula, lecturer slides, execution instructions and evaluation results have been published in the form of a handbook.

Best practice

Analysis and preparation of 10 best practice cases on the promotion of labour market participation by women and older people, especially from Denmark, Sweden, Norway and Finland and transfer to the countries south of the Baltic Sea. The specific national conditions were investigated in order to allow implementation in the recipient countries.

The analysis of the conditions for the transfer of best practices and the 10 best practices have been published in the Baltic Sea Academy series of publications.

Regional/national cooperations

Drafting and completion of memoranda of understanding on promoting innovative SMEs through women's entrepreneurship, and the increased employment of women and older people in Latvia, Lithuania, Belarus, North Poland and North Germany.

The memoranda containing the support activities to be implemented by the signatory institutions have been published in a manual.

Strategy programme

Strategic programme to promote innovation and the labour market participation of women and older people in SMEs as well as to increase the attractiveness of regional labour markets.

The strategy programme and two action plans (see below) were published as part of the Baltic Sea Academy series of publications.

Action plans

In order to involve 50 economic chambers and 16 universities in all the Baltic Sea countries in promoting the employment of women and older people in SMEs on a permanent basis, two action programmes have been developed and enacted:

a) action programme for 50 SME promoters (chambers + associations) in all BSR countries on promoting higher labour market participation by women and older people and, thus, increasing innovation capacities in SMEs;

b) action programme for 16 academies/universities from 9 Baltic Sea countries on the promotion and qualification of consultants to support the labour market participation of women and older people.

The action plans and appendix were published alongside the strategy programme (see above) in the Baltic Sea Academy series of publications.

International consultancy and transfer conferences

In order to achieve the highest possible and sustainable implementation of the target project results across all the Baltic Sea Countries, in 2013 and 2014 written transfer was supported by two consultancy and transfer conferences lasting several days with representatives from all the Baltic Sea countries. All the presentations and consultancy results developed were published in the Baltic Sea Academy series of publications in the following articles:

a) Corporate Social Responsibility and Women`s Entrepreneurship around the Mare Balticum.

b) Innovative SMEs by Gender and Age around the Mare Balticum.

Country-specific activities

During the project, it became clear that there was a need for more in-depth, further-reaching work in some countries to the south of the Baltic Sea. The following additional activities were also carried out to cover this:

Germany

Analysis of businesswomen in Germany, including a survey.

Poland

a) organisation and evaluation of a conference on "Development of the competitiveness of enterprises in the context of demographic challenges";

b) analysis and elaboration on the employment of women and older people and its promotion;

c) analysis of women's activities in SMEs in Poland and scenarios for possible future development.

Lithuania

Theoretical analytical study of political activities: Building the socially responsible enployment policy in Baltic states

The results of these five additional activities were published in the Baltic Sea Academy series of publications.

Manual

Development and publication of a manual on promoting innovation through increasing the labour market participation of women and older people and the proportion of female entrepreneurs in SMEs.

The manual containing all the project results and additional tools for the management of demographic change at enterprise level has been published as part of the Baltic Sea Academy series of publications under the title "Manual - Innovative SMEs by Gender and Age in the Baltic Sea Region."

This book incorporates the report of „Building the socially responsible employment policy in Baltic states", with a special focus on female entrepreneurs and elderly employees in Latvia and Lithuania.

Review by Dr. Misiūnas

The selection of scientific publications "Building the socially responsible employment policy in Baltic states"

The topic that is disclosed in the scientific publication "Building the socially responsible employment policy in Baltic states" is certainly relevant to the context of national economy and social policy. Experience shows that socially responsible employment policy measures are especially widely used in the old EU member states. Relevance of socially responsible employment policy is not decreasing because unfavourable economic conditions aggravate the employment of certain groups of people (especially the long-term unemployed, low-skilled, having low marketable professions and other persons). The content of scientific publications by the authors of this publication allows to answer reasonably to questions about the development of socially responsible employment policy in the Baltic states. The results of accomplished analysis are relevant to the fact that they allow to reveal the problems that are encountered in the development of socially responsible employment policy.

Creation of socially responsible employment policy is assessed in the publication through corporate social responsibility (CSR) development perspective. Particular attention is given to the development of responsible employment policy in A. Ignotas' publication "The development of the integration of population seeking to enter the labour market and entrepreneurship in Lithuania in the context of corporate social responsibility changes". Applying comparative analysis method, opportunities of integration into the labour market for women, men, the elderly, youth, and people with disabilities are assessed sufficiently in detail; these opportunities are not separable from the development issues of responsible employment policy.

The latter groups of persons have been attributed to the socially vulnerable target groups whose opportunities for successful integration into the labour market are problematic. However, characteristic of this publication is that priority was given to the target groups of women and the elderly; these target groups have its own specifics of the integration into the labour market and they are in need of responsible business support.

According to the reviewer, the authors of publications to a large extent were able to uncover it.

Various relevant ideas of socially responsible business and employment policy have been discussed in the publication. For example, development of socially responsible business is associated with the need to improve the quality of education of leading corporate staff themselves (leading professionals) in V. Bikse and B. Rivza's publication "Latvia's labour market trends and challenges for entrepreneurship education".

Weighty role of innovations in the country's structural changes of economy is revealed in another publication of scientists from Latvia (T. Volkova, I. Baranovska). An important conclusion could be drawn from the analysis that was reviewed by the authors of the article "The new meaning of innovations in the context of structural changes of economy" that more rapid implementation of the latter innovations could improve competitiveness, adaptability in the labour market and welfare of women and the elderly.

In addition to numerous analytical material, a set of research articles that was developed by the authors also includes interesting findings on a theoretical level. For example, an important and worthy of serious scientific discussion insight has been formulated in the publication; labour market flexibility is overly counterposed against employment security in labour market policy area, though their balance is declared. It is rightly pointed out in the publication that there is the need to change the conceptual approach to the very concept of labour market flexibility. The very flexibility of the labour market should be based precisely on CSR. CSR is a way to ensure labour market flexibility combining interests of employer and employee.

It is believed that despite the undoubted scientific importance and utility of prepared publication, in order to develop socially responsible business in the Baltic countries, a definite focus on contributing to a higher awareness among employers should be given in prospect; increase of awareness is a very important condition for the development of CSR helping more socially vulnerable members of population groups to integrate into the labour market. Of course, it can be argued what target groups are necessary to be distinguished forming socially responsible and successful employment policy. However, it already could be the object of other future scientific publications and researches, which could be further successfully developed by the authors of this publication.

11

The prepared publication is useful for scientists, professionals of various state institutions, the students of education process, business representatives and experts, whose activities and interests are related to the labour market problems, labour market policy and its implementation capabilities. In view of the stated arguments, the publication "Building the socially responsible employment policy in Baltic states" is recommended to be printed.

Ph.D. of Social science Algimantas Misiūnas

Review by Prof. Dr. Rutkauskas

The selection of scientific publications "Building the socially responsible employment policy in Baltic states"

Relevant economic social employment topics of specific target groups in the labour market in Baltic states are systematically examined in the selection of scientific articles that are interdependent in common themes "Building the socially responsible employment policy in Baltic states". It is generally recognized in scientific publications and practical activities that there is still a lack of comprehensive, consistent researches, as well as detailed systematic statistical data reflecting the situation and the dynamics of different vulnerable groups of persons in the labour market.

Theoretically, it is very well that authors of these scientific articles systematically newly formulate these employment topics in a social responsibility aspect. The results of scientific, analytical studies confirm that socially responsible employment policy measures (especially the ones of the southern Baltic states) are not sufficiently efficient and not sufficiently effectively realizable in pursuance of socially responsible business in enterprise (especially small and medium-sized) level.

The relevance of socially responsible employment policy, which is integrated in public institutions and the enterprise level, is not decreasing and the effectiveness of its implementation should be essentially increased. The content of the scientific publications in this selection of Lithuanian and Latvian authors allows on the scientific basis to more fully answer to questions about socially responsible employment policy development in the Baltic states, enables to define the existing primary obstacles of the integration of the target groups into employment, thus referring in which manner implementers of the different level of social and employment policy would most effectively contribute to these integration processes.

The implementation of socially responsible employment policy is related to a complex of factors under consideration in a selection of articles. Those factors are the economic situation, social and cultural environment, traditions of social security, education and vocational training, the degree of tolerance in the society, territorial economic features, the degree of sociality, the perception of social solidarity in society and others.

Socially responsible employment policy making is described in more detail in dr. A. Ignotas' publication "The development of the integration of population seeking to enter the labour market and entrepreneurship in Lithuania in the context of corporate social responsibility changes". Opportunities of integration into the labour market for women, men, the elderly, youth and people with disabilities are assessed in a selection of the articles; these opportunities are not separable from formation and implementation of socially responsible employment policy.

Relevant ideas of Latvian socially responsible business and realizable employment policy are also discussed in the publication. T. Volkova, I. Baranovska reveals valid role of innovations in the country's structural changes of economy. A conclusion is made in their research paper "The new meaning of innovations in the context of structural changes of economy"; the conclusion says that faster implementation of innovations could improve competitiveness of women and the elderly, their adaptability in the labour market. Effectiveness of socially responsible business development is examined assessing education quality of managers in companies in V. Bikse and B. Rivza's publication "Latvia's labour market trends and challenges for entrepreneurship education".

In summary, it can be reasonably stated that prepared selection of scientific articles will no doubt be useful for scientists, professionals in public administration institutions, business representatives and experts, whose activity is related to labour market problems and policy. The publication "Building the socially responsible employment policy in Baltic states" is recommended to be printed.

Prof. habil. dr. Aleksandras Vytautas Rutkauskas

Vilnius Gediminas Technical University

Enhancement of Opportunities for Economic Activities of Elderly People in Lithuania

Vytas Navickas

Similar to other EU countries, unfavourable tendencies in the labour market approached from a long-term perspective have been observed in Lithuania as well. The most essential changes are related to a decrease in supply of labour force. This has been conditioned by natural changes in birth rates and dynamics of structural tendencies in labour force.

From this perspective, a significant influence on intensity of labour force supply has been predetermined by a considerable drop in the indicators of economic activity of elderly people.

The analysis of demographic data in Lithuania reveals an obvious process of ageing of the population and the topicality of finding ways to cope with its consequences. According to the data of Lithuanian Department of Statistics, in the beginning of 2011 there were 701,200 people of 60 years old and over, which made up 21.6 % of all the population. During 2010 the number of such people increased by 4,100 (0.6 %), whereas over the last 10 years this number has risen by 32,600 individuals (4.9 %).
Intensive emigration of employable people from Lithuania also has also contributed to the complicated situation in the labour market at present.

Dynamics of numbers of emigrants from Lithuania, changes in immigration (in thousands)

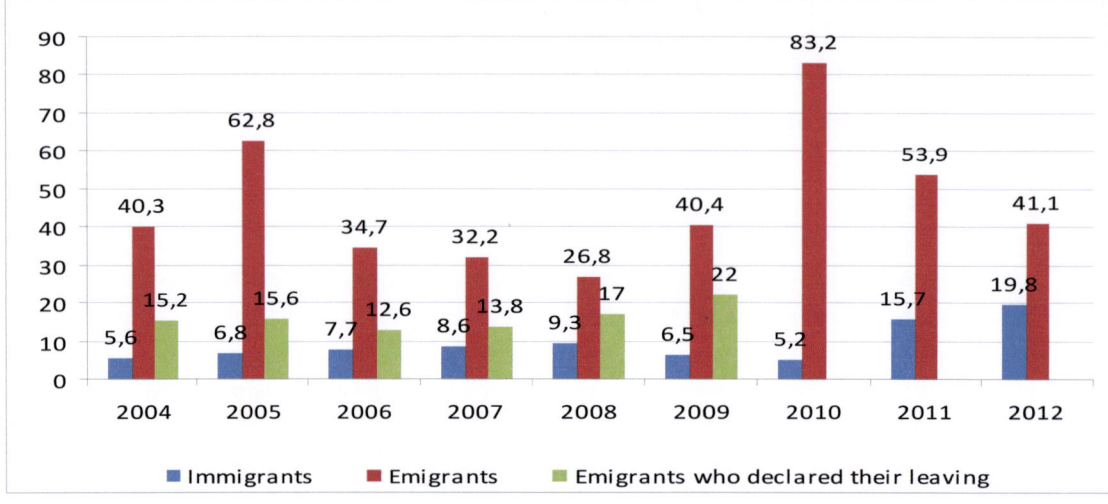

Source: revised data of the Department of Statistics

Therefore, the perspectives of labour market should be closer linked to assurance of long-term employment activities among elderly people.

Over the last three years the average life expectancy of elderly men and women has slightly increased. Women, who turned 60 years old in 2010 are expected to live on the average another 22.3 years, whereas men are likely to live another 16.2 years (in 2007 this indicator was 21.7 years for women and 15.4 for men).

On the basis of the forecast provided by the Statistical Office of the European Union (Eurostat), a fast ageing of the populating in Lithuania is foreseen. It has been calculated that in the beginning of 2060 almost 37 % of the Lithuanian population will be elderly people and the average of the 27 states of the European Union (hereinafter – EU) will total 35 percent.

Lithuanian population according to gender and age (2013 and forecast of 2060)

In the beginning of the year

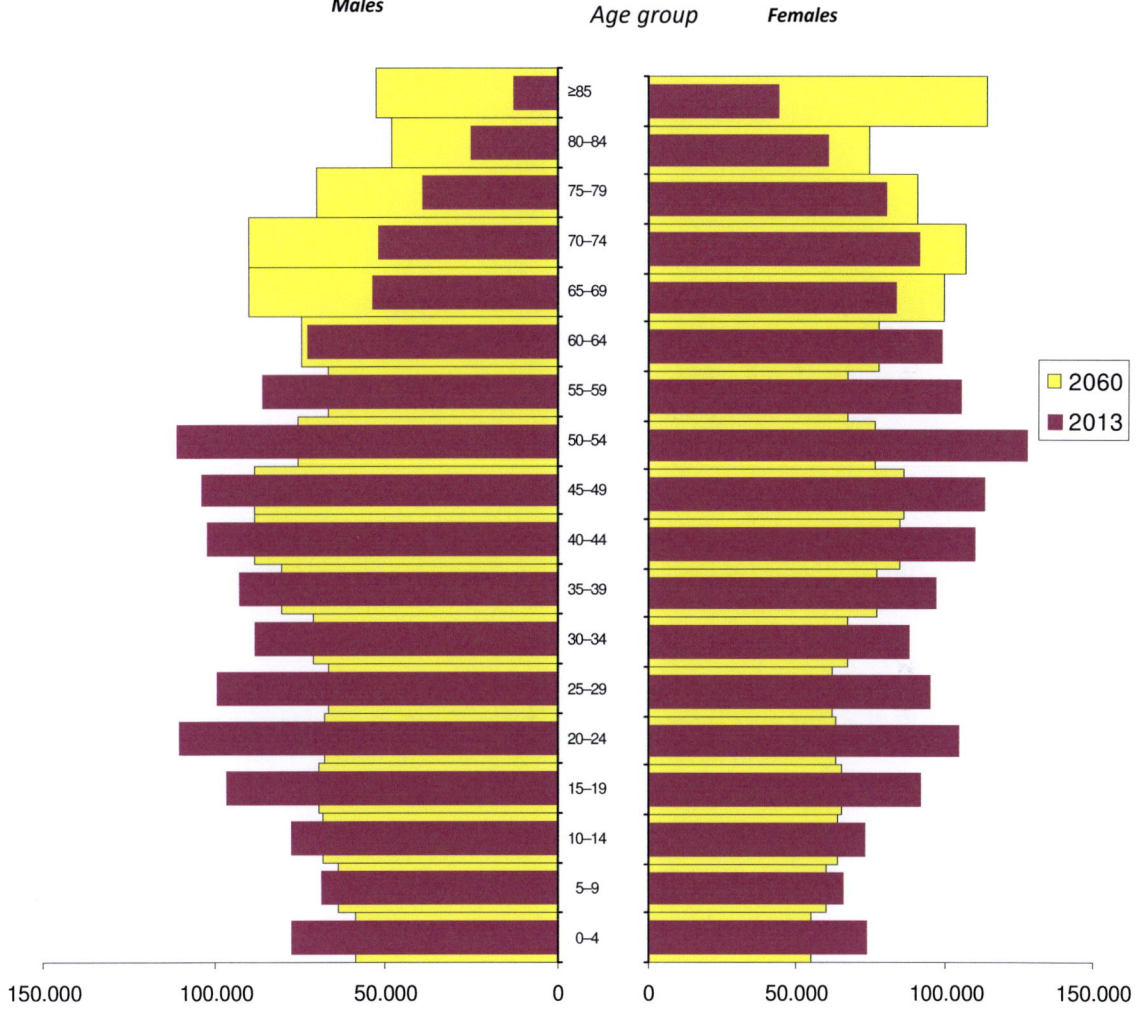

Source : *Eurostat's database (16 January 2014).*

Prior to 2010 about 50,000 new people used to enter the labour market every year. However, in 2011 this number underwent a considerable downfall. During the nearest 15–20 years the number of employable people will further go down. The bottom will be hit, when children, who are currently 6–8 years old, embark on their working career. The number of children of this generation totals 30 000 individuals. Then the real bottom will be felt. The numbers of representatives of younger generations are as twice as low compared to those of generations born in the period of 1950–1990.

Ageing of population is a complex phenomenon, which results in various social and economic consequences; therefore, it is important to search for solutions how to avoid problems deriving from ageing of population and to employ opportunities that emerge because of increase in the duration of employable age of population. This phenomenon should be considered while formulating economic, social and employment policy. The problem of ageing has been included into the national priorities in Lithuania.

The National Strategy for Overcoming Population Aging Outcomes was approved in Lithuania. It states that following the principles of active ageing, elderly people should be provided with conditions for full-value life, their experience should be appreciated and they have to be sure of their future. The measures for implementation of this Strategy have also been provided for.

The problem of ageing population is analysed in the Programme of the Government of the Republic of Lithuania in the context of social and family issues. The programme provides for plans to improve the system of social insurance, to initiate increase in pension, to create more efficient system of social support provision, to improve provision of social care and services, to strengthen the sense of communality and solidarity of generations.

The problems of elderly people have also been addressed in other national strategic documents. The National Strategy of Demographic (Population) Policy provides for long-term aims, objectives and actions of demographic policy, which are related to solutions of ageing-related problems through improvement of quality of health and social services to elderly people.

The Interdisciplinary Activity Plan for Promotion of Non-discrimination for 2012-2014 embraces various educative events, promotion of activities of non-governmental activities, which would contribute to decreasing of discrimination on various bases including the age as well.

The National Programme of Equal Opportunities for 2010-2014 sets out provisions for prevention of any manifestations of gender-based discrimination, which are also important while ensuring non-discrimination of elderly people.

The Programme for Minimizing of Social and Economic Differences of Regions provides for measures, which are targeted at solutions to unequal development of social infrastructure, low level of economic activity in rural areas, low attractiveness of living environment of a number of towns and, thus, contribute to solving of social problems caused by ageing of the society.

 Attempts are made to better finance systems of social security and to ensure that during the economic boom the income of elderly people meets the level of growth in the national welfare. On the other hand, during the period of economic recession or crisis, the financial situation of elderly people should not experience unproportional decline.

To attain the aforesaid goal, the Parliament approved the Guidelines for the Reform of the State Social Insurance and Pension System.

The measures that strengthen elderly people's chances to remain in the labour market introducing new means of active labour market policy. EU funds are used to achieve the aforesaid goals as well as projects initiated by local governments. Considerable attention is allocated to increase of social inclusion.

 Though passive measures for assurance of life quality are rather important, they do not compensate social, emotional and economic motivational stimuli of full-value life provided by professional activity to elderly people, who are able to take part in the labour market.

Economic migration of employable people and world economic financial crisis necessitate search for the balance between challenges to nearest ageing policy and possible challenges in further perspective.

Taking into account the above-mentioned circumstances and addressing challenges of the ageing process, it is necessary to improve the quality of elderly people's life: to increase their incomes, to improve living environment, the range and accessibility of health care services as well as to introduce other measures, which contribute to promotion of economic activity of elderly people.

Enhancement of entrepreneurship, and particularly entrepreneurship of elderly people, are of utmost importance addressing problems of economic activity.

During the survey carried out in Lithuania, the main spheres, which stimulate elderly people's economic activity, were identified.

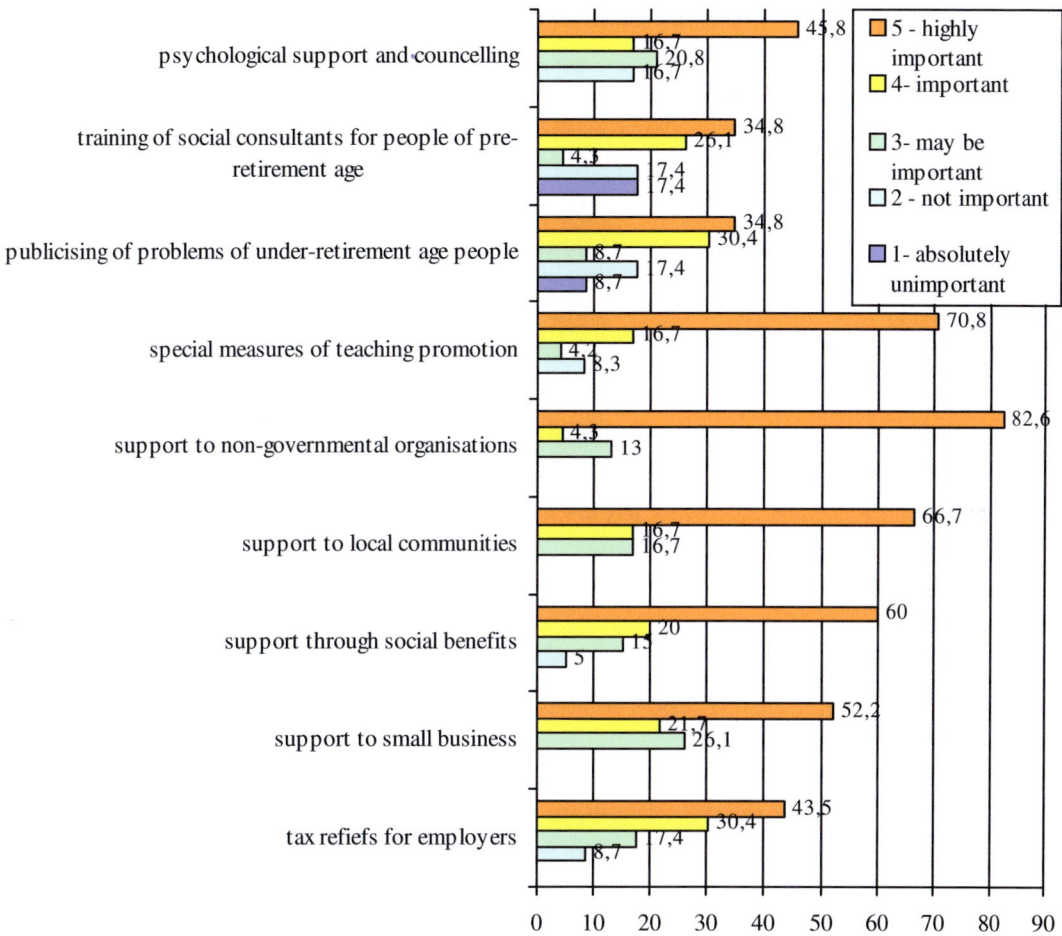

The survey revealed that elderly people are ready to involve in the process of learning (various study programmes). To improve the system of vocational training, the respondents suggest tuning the study programmes with the needs of the labour market, to forecast the demand for certain professions and to more flexibly adapt to requirements of the market.

More than half of the respondents expressed their wish to learn foreign languages and to acquire computer skills. A number of the respondents pointed out that while organising vocational training for elderly individuals it is necessary to consider their age and ability to assume new information. The bigger part of the respondents think that education for elderly people should be free.

Organising non-formal education, it is also important to take into account the age, health condition, kinds of diseases and wish of elderly people. The majority of the respondents expressed a wish to attend courses of healthy lifestyle. However, it was noticed that there is a lack of methodological material for implementation of programmes for health promotion: it is necessary to write and publish books and various publications on this issue.

The respondents also think that while improving the employment opportunities of elderly people, the mechanism of encouraging employers to recruit elderly people should be improved, collaboration between the labour exchange and employers should be improved and flexible forms of work should be applied. The respondents also point out that close collaboration of labour exchange, employers and non-governmental organisations is particularly important.

The respondents also provided recommendations about improvement of activities of non-governmental organisations (trade unions, organisations of elderly people and others). They stated that it is necessary to strengthen collaboration of these organisations as well as to promote dissemination of experience among these organisations.
A big number of the respondents noticed that non-governmental or community organisations should inform elderly people regarding employment of senior citizens, to organise meeting with consultants and specialists in various spheres.

However, as it can be concluded from the data of the survey, a number of the respondents think (20.8 %) that the aforesaid organisations should focus on issues related to non-economic activity of elderly people (culture, organisation of leisure activities, health promotion). Moreover, the majority of the respondents pointed out that community organisations should receive financing from the budget.

According to the experts in elderly people, financial and legal measures (tax reliefs, subsidies, preferential loans) should be provided for to encourage employers to recruit elderly people. Such measures would encourage elderly people to involve in small business.

In fact the majority of the respondents understand that successful professional activities require proper vocational preparation. Thus, education systems should meet requirements of labour market and national/regional economy, newest technologies, health condition and their professional training of elderly people.

The promotion of economic activity is of importance to the whole labour market of the EU. This has been confirmed by the data of Eurostat research.

Economically inactive population is a bigger problem that the unemployed. Since 2002 and despite the economic crisis, the share of the inactive population in the total population of working age has fallen from 31.4 % to 28.3 % in the EU-28. This corresponds to a reduction of 7.9 million inactive persons. The decline in inactivity rates is mainly due to the rising participation of women in the labour force.

The share of women outside the labour market fell during that period by 5 percentage points, from 39.6 % to 34.5 %, while the share of men outside the labour force decreased by only 1 percentage point (from 23.2 % in 2002 to 22.1 % in 2012). As a consequence, the gender gap decreased continuously in the EU during this period of time, from 16.4 % in 2002 to 12.4 % in 2012.

The trends of economic activities in the Lithuanian labour market are similar to those of the EU

Level of labour force activity (15-64 years old) %

	2008	2009	2010	2011*	2012*
Total (15-64 yo)	68.4	69.8	70.5	71.4	71.9
Women	65.5	67.8	68.8	69.3	70.1
Men	71.4	72.0	72.4	73.6	73.8
Youth (15-24 yo)	30.8	30.3	29.6	28.1	29.3

This decreasing pattern in the inactivity rate hides very contrasting situations depending on the age group. More than 50 % of men and women aged 15-24 are inactive. This high number is explained by the fact that many young people are still in education or training.

Looking at the trend over the last decade, while the inactivity rate of women aged 15-24 has remained very stable (close to 60 %), the inactivity rate of men aged 15-24 has increased, in particular since 2009 and the onset of the crisis. Looking at the age group 55-64, more than 40 % of men and women are inactive.

This population has, however, experienced the strongest decrease since 2002, mostly explained by the widespread adoption of policies to promote active ageing. The inactivity rate of men aged 55-64 fell by 10 % (from 49 % in 2002 to 39 % in 2012) and by 14 % for women (from 69 % in 2002 to 55 % in 2012). The category 25-54 is by far the biggest of the three groups in terms of population, but it is also the age group experiencing the lowest inactivity rates. In this group, the inactivity rate of men is stable at a very low level (8 % in 2012). The inactivity rate of women aged 25-54 is continuously decreasing, but remains very high compared to that of men.

The consequence of very high inactivity rates for young and old people is even more visible in absolute figures, with a number of inactive persons being similar in the three age groups: in the EU-28 in 2012, the age group 15-24 encompasses 33 million inactive people out of a total of 57.5 million people. In the age group 25-54, 31.1 million persons out of 211.6 million were inactive. Finally, 30 million persons out of 63.4 million were inactive in the age group 55-64.

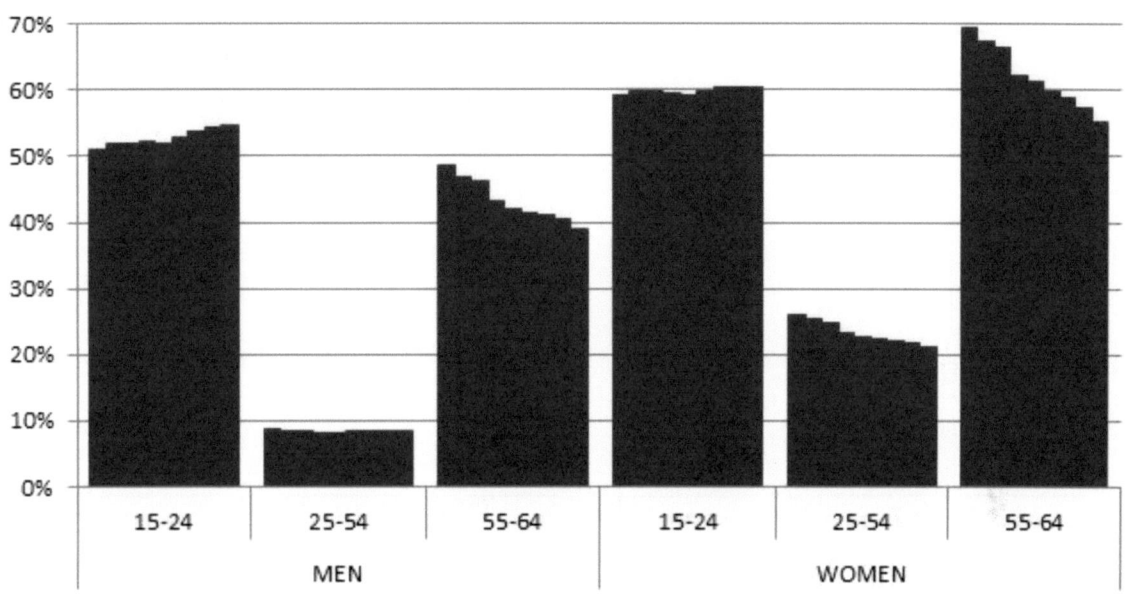

Source: Eurostat

Another determining factor of inactivity is the educational level attained. Persons attaining a low educational level are more likely to be inactive. In 2012 and for the whole EU-28, the inactivity rate of persons in the age group 25-64 who had attained a low educational level (i.e. less than lower secondary) was 36.6 %, as compared to 20.6 % for persons with a medium educational level (at least lower secondary level, but less than tertiary) and 11.6 % for persons with a high (i.e. tertiary) level. This means that the likelihood of staying out of the labour market is more than 3 times greater for the poorly educated than for highly-educated people. This relationship between education and inactivity applies irrespective of sex and age.

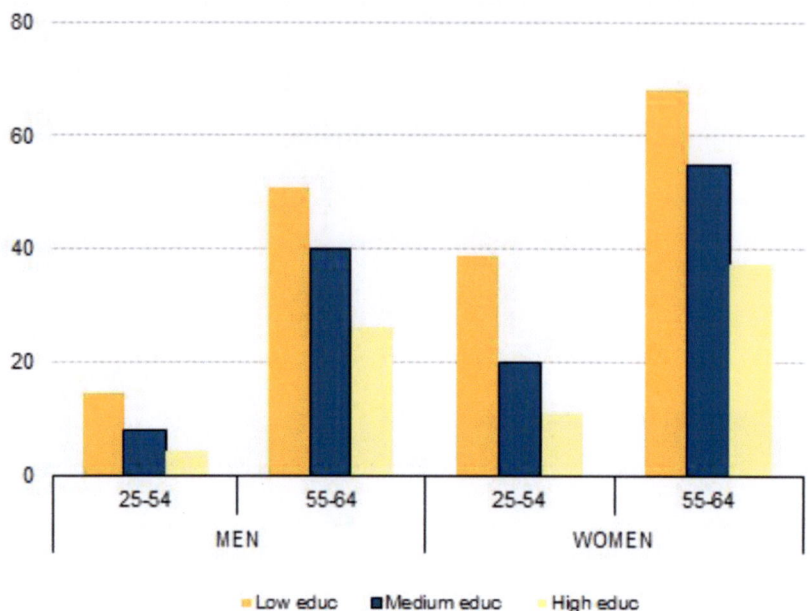

Source: Eurostat

The reasons for economic inactivity of elderly people are various. It is frequently conditioned by physical disability, a wish to have more free time for trying out of other aspects of life, the financial situation, which allows to maintain sufficiently high quality of life without employment, situation in the family and others. In the context of the EU, Lithuania belongs to the group of countries, where the most considerable factor is the retirement age, when individuals become economically inactive.

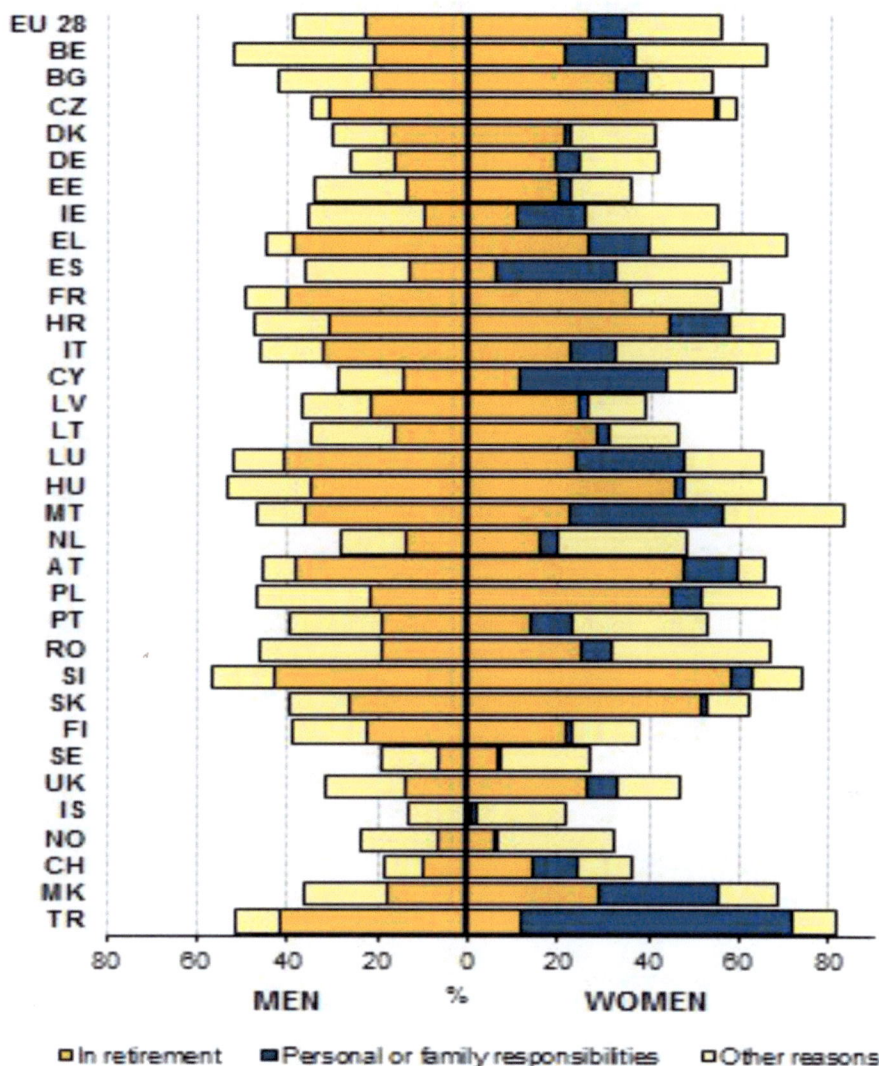

Inactivity rates of older persons (55-64) by sex and main reason for not looking for a job, 2012 , Source: Eurostat

Strengthening of economic activity of senior people should be conducted in an integrated way. This embraces not only assurance of longer period of employment but also solutions to the problem of social harmony of different generations, transformation of managerial functions of business and establishment of more favourable conditions for self-dependent economic activity.

At present the majority of private business enterprises in Lithuania are established by 30-40 year old individuals. It should also be mentioned that since 2011 the number of 50 year old and older men, who create private business, has decreased, whereas the number of women of this age group, who have founded their own business, has remained almost the same.

Therefore, the enhancement of attention to this sphere is necessary. What are the main trends for provision of more favourable conditions for business activities of elderly people?

The extensive research has been carried out on this issue. Generalising the acquired results, it can be pointed out that better perspectives for this group of labour force would be ensured if work assignments were more individualised, more flexible timetables of work and rest were devised, mentoring programmes were more intensively implemented, provision of services of information and consultation were enhanced and specialised economic stimuli were applied to encourage elderly people to be in employment. This would be useful not only in terms of financial results but would also contribute to implementation of initiatives that support entrepreneurship development.

It is particularly important to point out that the 50-plus generation has accumulated valuable experience for business establishment and frequently possesses necessary education.

The countries, where conditions for setting up of business as well as general economic situation are more favourable, the factor of education is not seen as relevant in the beginning of establishing business. On the contrary, in the countries, which have only recently started encouraging and promoting entrepreneurship (e.g., in Lithuania), relationships, previous experience and education are more important.

Over 60 % of individuals, who start their own business or carry out activities on the basis of business licence, have higher education. Though the number of entrepreneurs without higher education has been increasing, there are few top managers without higher education.

More than half of the people in Lithuania, who are establishing new businesses, point out that they have previously worked in other companies. Among the individuals who have set up their own businesses, 12 % of women worked in top positions in their previous workplaces, whereas there were 32 % of such men. Moreover, Lithuania's indicator of male executives, who have accumulated useful experience and have established useful contacts in other enterprises, differs from the EU average (18 %) significantly.

More active strengthening of entrepreneurship of elderly people would contribute to strategic goals aimed at entrepreneurship promotion in the EU.

However, the spirit of entrepreneurship (it is an indicator of potential or more active establishment of workplaces) is weaker in the EU compared to other developed countries. Only 11 % of the Europeans are entrepreneurs and about 40 % seek for self-employment. In the USA and Chine more than half of the population want to be self-employed.

The Programme of the Lithuanian Employment Policy provides for important measures to strengthen entrepreneurship and to solve topical problems of the labour market employing it.

Summary

The article discusses the programmes of promotion of economic activities of elderly people in Lithuania and measures provided for in the strategic documents of Lithuania and the EU. The perspectives of the labour market as well as its structural changes are also analysed. The author discusses the most important measures for promotion of economic activities of elderly people and the necessity for structural changes in social services.

Literature

1. Action plan 'Entrepreneurship 2020',European Commission,2013
2. Nacionalinė Europos vyresnio amžiaus žmonių aktyvumo ir kartų solidarumo metų programa. Socialinės apsaugos ministerija, 2012
3. Pagyvenusių asmenų mokymosi ir užimtumo didinimo veiksmų planas .Darbo ir socialinių tyrimų institutas,2003
4. Eurostat. Unemployment statstics.http://epp.eurostat.ec.europa.eu/statistics_explained/index.php/Unemployment_statistics

About Autor

Prof. Dr. Vytas Navickas

Economist – mathematician study at Vilnius University; Doctor. Research worker in Institute of Economy at Academy of Science; Head of Economic Reform Division in Ministry Council 1989-1990; Director JSC" Draudos autocentras"-Representative DaimlerChrysler AG in Lithuania; Member of the Seimas of the Republic of Lithuania 2004-2008; Minister of Economy of the Republic of Lithuania in five Governments 1990-1991,1995-1996,2006-2008, Professor and Dean at the Lithuanian University of educational sciences, Faculty of Social Sciences.

The Integration of the Population Seeking to Enter the Labour Market and Corporate Social Responsibility

Anicetas Ignotas

Lithuanian University of Educational Sciences, Department of Economics

The aim of this article is to evaluate state of corporate social responsibility (CSR) in Lithuania and the observed changes in this area. This paper also provides an overview of CSR experience in formation of traditions and their development in individual country's business enterprises, and discusses the role of companies for responsible business formation. The article also identifies the factors that led to the development of CSR in the country. One of the main priorities of the analysis of the integration of the country's population into the labour market is assessment of the situation of the self-employed persons (having their business) in the country under separate population groups (women, the elderly) and place of residence. This analysis reveals differences of entrepreneurship in the country through the assessment of changes in the structure of employees by employment status. Much attention is also paid to the assessment of the application opportunities of flexible forms of employment, highlighting the status of women through applying these forms. Statistics Lithuania (further Department of Statistics) and Eurostat data and other sources of information (the results of separate surveys) are used in this article.

Keywords: *corporate social responsibility, integration, labour market, entrepreneurship, employment status.*

Introduction

Responsible business development in separate companies of the country is closely linked to the increase of attractiveness of their employees' employment. Nevertheless, job-creation and the realization of opportunities for the promotion of entrepreneurship reflect CSR development tendencies. Most of the information about CSR in Lithuania reflect the formal ("front") CSR side, but relevant studies, which would reflect real and unvarnished situation in the country, are especially lacking. The most noteworthy study is the study "Corporate Social Responsibility Trends among Small and Medium-sized Enterprises in the Baltic Countries", which emphasizes that only 43.6 percent chiefs of country's small and medium-sized companies did not know what corporate (general) social responsibility is. Moreover, the results of the study showed that 52 percent country's small and medium-sized enterprises are not yet implemented any CSR program. 37.7 percent companies claimed that they had carried out CSR activities. 54.9 percent of them said that they are carrying out CSR activities for more than three years, 25.2 percent – about two years, and 19.9 percent – about one year. On the other hand, the extent of CSR development in the country is far from sufficient judging by slowly pending problems of unemployment and the relatively low level of well-being, which could be reached by the people working in Lithuania.

It is clear that CSR development is concurrent with the creation of jobs the solution of employment problems in different sectors of the economy. Employment has become the absolute priority by the revised Lisbon Strategy. This was reflected during the period of programming the Community financial instruments for the period 2007-2013 (Community Programme of Employment and Social Solidarity, the European Social Fund and European Regional Development Fund). At the same time, the European Commission is supporting the fight against unemployment and undeclared work by modernizing the public employment services and by encouraging flexibility of employers and employees. It promotes the use of different policy approaches considering the key economic sectors, such as services, and categories of workers that can be better integrated into the labour market (such as women and the elderly).[1] CSR development involves various areas which are associated with job-creation and their maintenance.

More rapid realization of opportunities for CSR development in Lithuania determines trends of integration of the population, which pursues to anchor in the labour market, and trends of entrepreneurship changes. Maintenance of skilled labour resources in the open labour market in Lithuania depends on the latter changes. The acceleration of real CSR development by increasing the attractiveness of the labour is one of the most important ways that can reduce the large migration flows of the working-age population from Lithuania. If high long-term emigration of skilled workers remained, Lithuania would suffer huge economic losses which would occur in its economic development slowdown of rates. The latter remarks determine the relevance of this article.

---

[1]http://europa.eu/legislation_summaries/employment_and_social_policy/job_creation_measures/index_lt.htm.

The Assessment of Opportunities for the Development of Corporate Social Responsibility and their Role in Responsible Business Formation and Factors Influencing the Situation

Experience shows that the traditions of CSR are deeply rooted in Western Europe. Accession of countries to the EU encouraged the development of CSR in the new EU member states. On the other hand, it can be said that the focus on problems of CSR development did not bypass countries from other continents. For example, problems of CSR and the situation of the development in the Middle East[2], Peru[3], and Africa[4]are analyzed in the separate publications.CSR can be counterposed against one-sided pursuit of profit at the economy entity level. However, only the development of CSR comprehensively combining interests of the business and the public can help to create long-term well-being of people living in a state.

Talking of Lithuania it is important to emphasize that CSR at national policy level in the website of Ministry of Social Security and Labour is defined as an ideology, policy, and practice of companies, reflecting such behaviour of companies, when they voluntarily involve social and environmental issues into their activities and they are guided by the codes of the respect for the individual, society and the environment in relations with all interested representatives of society, business and government.[5] In other words, CSR is policy and practice of companies, when they voluntarily integrate social, environmental and transparent business principles into internal processes and external relationships of their activity in accordance with the laws, international agreements and agreed norms of behaviour. Companies with social and public sector partners are looking for innovative, systemic and broader solutions to social, environmental and economic well-being problems.[6]

---

[2]Ehaab A. Nelson J., Fahmy A., Greenwald D. *The Status and Potential of Social Entrepreneurship in the Middle East. Brookings Institution* (April 27, 2010).
[3]Rees C., Kemp D, and Davis R. _Conflict Management and Corporate Culture in the Extractives Sector: A Study in Peru_. CSRI Report No. 50. (September, 2012).
[4]Forstater M., Zadek S, Guang Y, Yu K., Xiao C., George H.M. *Corporate Resposibility in African Development Insigrhts from an Emergening Dialog.* CSRI Working Paper No. 60 (October, 2010).
[5]Ministry of Social Security and Labour(http://www.socmin.lt/index.php?1665385471).
[6]http://europa.eu/youreurope/business/environment/energy-labels/index_lt.htm#lithuania_lt_taking-sustainability-further.

On the other hand, the legal side of CSR is more emphasized in the European Commission's definition. CSR refers to companies voluntarily going beyond what the law requires to achieve social and environmental objectives during the course of their daily business activities. Corporate social responsibility covers a range of areas:

- Europe 2020 (especially new skills and jobs, youth, local development),
- business and human rights,
- corporate social responsibility reporting,
- socially responsible public procurement.[7]

EU corporate social responsibility has been associated with economic, social and environmental objectives of the Lisbon strategy, because it is believed that the enterprises using the corporate social responsibility will contribute to job creation and the improvement of working conditions, security of workers' rights, the development of science and technological innovation.[8] The development of national policies and the development peculiarities of individual EU countries are available in various sources (see the source in brackets[9]).

The opinion is offered that CSR is principles of companies' activity (CSR). The latter principles actually involve separate areas of activity of CSR which were previously listed by the European Commission definition with a special emphasis on business representatives who need to take into account interests of stakeholders (consumers, employees, community, business representatives, government, society, etc.).[10] In this way, the importance of harmonization of interests of different population groups is accentuated in CSR activities that the objectives of business would not be against (would not be opposed to) interests of society and would serve all people's welfare.

As already mentioned, data of the study "General Trends of Social Responsibility among Small and Medium-sized Enterprises in the Baltic Countries" may be enough to

---

[7]European Commission (http://ec.europa.eu/social/main.jsp?catId=331&langId=lt).

[8]The Program of the Development of Corporate Social Responsibility for 2009-2013 and Plan of Measures for its Implementation in 2009-2011.

[9]Corporate Social Responsibility National public policies in the European Union (07/05/2008). http://ec.europa.eu/social/main.jsp?catId=331&langId=en&pubId=61&type=2&furtherPubs=yes.

[10]http://vkc.vtf.lt/apieISA.

critically evaluate the CSR situation and changes of situation in Lithuania. On the other hand, there is a lack of the direct studies of the actual situation of CSR in Lithuania. However, the situation can be assessed from other studies that are closely related to the assessment of environmental factors of the favourable development of CSR. Social cohesion is one of the most important factors which shapes such environment; close social relationships and trust in various institutions determine the social cohesion. For example, the study from the German Research Center "Bertelsmann Foundation" shows that social cohesion in Lithuania is weak. It is not possible to achieve a high level of development, which is based on long-term traditions of development of CSR, without the purposeful formation of social cohesion in the country. Lithuania overtakes only four countries – Latvia, Bulgaria, Greece and Romania in aforesaid study "Bertelsmann Foundation", which evaluated the strength of cohesion of 34 countries of the European Union and the Organization of Economic Cooperation and Development. According to the study, the strongest cohesion is in the Scandinavian countries – Denmark, Norway, Sweden and Finland. Indicators of confidence in people and identification with the nation, social networks and acceptance of diversity were improved in Lithuania, while civic participation has fallen considerably over two decades.[11]

Notices of the experts who evaluated examples of good practice of the responsible business can be used in default of the data of sociological researches, which would thoroughly evaluate CSR developments in Lithuania. For example, the National Responsible Business Award jury members (latter jury members are purposefully considered serious experts with competence in the situation in Lithuania), who pointed out quite a few positive CSR development assessments, presented and the serious criticisms for responsible business development problems.An opinion is offered that responsible business is just beginning in Lithuania. Companies often value socially responsible activities as a tool to promote their products or services. Yet not many companies understand that long-term CSR activities would bring real benefits.An important role falls to the media during the spread of CSR ideas: journalists should publicly publish whether reports of companies correspond to reality. However, there is no doubt that the CSR movement will expand in Lithuania (*Human Rights Monitoring Institute director Henrikas Mickevičius*). The largest prophets of social responsibility are foreign capital companies coming to Lithuania, and employers' organizations of Lithuania are too little aware of corporate social responsibility philosophy and principles. The activities of

---

[11]Study: Weak Social Cohesion in Lithuania. http://m.alfa.lt/naujienos/Lietuva/28470/.

Lithuanian business organizations are mainly focused on lobbying in the Parliament and the Government, the rapid pursuit of profit (*Trade Union of Lithuanian Food Producers chairman Gražina Gruzdienė*).

A number of other factors that strongly influence the opportunities of CSR development in Lithuania can be named. It must be emphasized that the majority of their effect depends on favour of economic development. The factors promoting the development of CSR are more evidenced during the good economic time, and the impact of the negative factors intensifies under the conditions of the economic crisis.

Key factors encouraging the development of Lithuanian CSR are:

- Long-term and sustainable growth of the economy;

- Fostering the socially responsible business traditions, developing enterprise network, and enhancing the part of socially responsible companies in the total businesses;

- Exciting increase in the number of jobs in the national economy;

- The growth of wages and labor productivity;

- Improvement in the labor market over a longer period of time (reduction of unemployment);

- Follow-up and consistent Lithuanian labor market integration in the EU labor market;

- Realization of expected Europe-2020 aspirations on the labor market and social protection;

- More favorable labor taxation policies and other potential incentives of attractive jobs.

Factors hindering the development of CSR in companies:

- An uneven development of economy cycles is associated with the negative impact of the economic crisis in the country and its regional social development;

- Job losses and the unfavorable change. Low development of fascinating jobs;

- Negative low wages paying traditions, relatively low labor productivity and minimum wage;

- A bad situation in the labor market and high unemployment;

- The large territorial disparities in unemployment and significant differences in the development of different regions;

- The existence of high social and economic development gap between the new EU countries and the EU old-timers;

- The impact of negative shadow economy and corruption relations on the country's most sustainable business development, lack of competitiveness;

- The dominant small entities (especially in peripheral regions) yet poorly take responsible business traditions.

Despite the existing problems, CSR traditions have been quite rapidly developed in Lithuania over the last decade. The state authorities and the proactive companies of the country have contributed significantly to it. Promotion of socially responsible business in Lithuania was carried out by using the selection of the best companies in this field and the bestowal of awards. There are different award categories for socially responsible business in Lithuania: the workplace of the year, the most communal enterprise of the year, the environment enterprise of the year, the socially responsible company of the year.

In order to promote the development of CSR in Lithuania, the Lithuanian National Responsible Business Network is established. In 2013 it operates and has members of 130 companies and organizations.[12] National Responsible Business Network members are large companies such as "Lietuva Statoil", "Mažeikių nafta", "Achemos grupė", „AGA", „Aviva Lietuva", Danisco Sugar Kėdainiai Panevėžys. While at the National CSR Network Lithuania has only 130 joined companies, but the popularity of the initiative is already growing. In particular, international companies follow the western country model to introduce CSR in the growing public pressure. It can be said that our country's growth

---

[12]http://www.socmin.lt/index.php?-2084770119.

potential of CSR is just beginning to gain momentum. The National Responsible Business Network (further – Network) was established in 2005.

The Network's mission is to promote the development of responsible business as a condition for sustainable development in Lithuania. Purpose of the Network is the exchange of information, experience and innovation, the organization of joint learning forums, the improvement of business strategies and the implementation of joint projects in the public interest. Companies and organizations which believe in sustainable development and responsible business respect workers' human and labor rights, protect the environment, resist corruption, are interested in developing strategies for sustainable business and civil society. These companies and organizations can become members of the Network formally acceding to the United Nations Global Compact initiative. The Network adopts and micro-enterprises, which are not listed in the UN Global Compact initiative. The Network runs completely a voluntary initiative. Initially, the Network was coordinated by the United Nations Development Programme (UNDP), but since 2007 the leadership of the Network training activities and meetings has been transferred to the company leader which changes every six month by a rotation. UNDP has an advisory role, provides expert support, coordinates key events in the Network with other CSR / Global Compact events in Lithuania and the region and serves as a link with the Global Compact Office.

The Development of Self-employment and Regional Differences

Due to the difficult financial situation in the country it is hardly possible to talk about the creation of new jobs in the public sector, therefore, only positive changes in the private sector can actually determine the increase in employment. However, most of jobs created for the wage labour in Lithuania are not sufficiently attractive concerning low-paid work and its adverse development trends. The average work payment grew very slowly in Lithuania even during the rapid improvement of the economic situation after the former economic crisis. Gross wages increased by only 4 percent according to data from the Department of Statistics (first-quarter of 2012 – 2138 LTL, first-quarter of 2013 – 2233 LTL). Quaterly real wage index through all 2012 (compared with the corresponding period of the previous year) was less than 100 percent. The latter trend shows the actual reduction in real work payment in Lithuania in the previous year, and it has grown at least several percents only in 2013 I-II quarter. The provisions to create one's own business seem more attractive under unfavourable trends of payment for work in the country, because income of the population seeking to establish themselves in the labour market in this way is highly dependent on their own efforts.

Successful CSR development in creating jobs is impossible without promotion of independent population employment. People having their own business, quite often not only create jobs for themselves, but also create opportunities to employ for other job seekers. Opportunities for the development of self-employment of population in Lithuania to a large extent can be forecasted by the situation of small and medium business (SMB). However, it was stated that the legal-economic environment is not favourable for small and medium business development in Lithuania: the unfinished reform of the legal system, remained bureaucratic business constraints, imperfect systems of bookkeeping and taxation, and so on.[13] Assessing opportunities of entrepreneurship in Lithuania, it should be taken into account that the economic development potential of the separate regions is very different. These factors force to take urgent measures that the situation for more continuous long-term economic development and reduction of disparities of development would be made in all regions in Lithuania, while improving environmental state and reducing the population differences in conditions of life, culture, and education.[14]

Judging from the official statistics, SMB and self-employment development problems have already accumulated over a relatively long period of time. In 2012, only about 125 thousand self-employed persons were in Lithuania. However, due to a lack of recalculated data in accordance with the results of population census (see the note under Table 1), it is difficult to compare absolute indicators of number of employed persons in dynamics until 2010, therefore, the analysis went by relative terms, which are appropriate to give priority assessing the situation over a longer period of time. Part of self-employed persons decreased from 16.8 to 9.7 percent in 1998-2012. The latter unfavourable trend can largely be explained by the fact that many jobs have been lost in independent business because of the decline in employment in agriculture until the economic crisis (until 2007), but one's own business was developed very slowly in other economic activities in Lithuania. Therefore, the overall balance of changes was negative. Nevertheless, the

---

[13]*Business Development in Lithuania and Eastern Europe.*Vilnius: Ministry of Economy of the Republic of Lithuania, Statistics Lithuania, 2000.
[14]Žukauskas R. S.*Smulkaus ir vidutinio verslo plėtros strateginės kryptys.* Public Policy and Administration, Vilnius 2002. No. 1.

absolute rate of self-employment has remained almost constant (about 65 thousand persons) in country's agriculture in 2008-2012, therefore, it can be said that during the economic crisis, small businesses have lost some jobs in other sectors of the economy.

Table 1

Employed by Their Status in Lithuania According to Data from Statistics Lithuania (in thousands)*

	1998	1999	2000	2001	2002	2003	2004	2005	2006	2007	2008	2009	2010	2011	2012
In total by status of employment	1489.4	1456.5	1397.8	1351.8	1405.9	1438	1436.3	1473.9	1499	1534.2	1520	1415.9	1247.7	1253.6	1275.7
Self-employed persons	251	234.2	233.6	218	233.3	242.8	216.7	206.3	199.8	183.2	152.9	146.3	115.6	115.2	124.3
Hired	1184.2	1164.4	1116	1090.9	1124	1144.8	1169.6	1224.1	1263.7	1324.4	1345	1244.8	1112	1120.8	1134.7
Contributory family members	54.2	58	48.2	42.9	48.6	50.4	49.9	43.5	35.5	26.7	22.1	24.7	20.1	17.5	16.7

* The population was recalculated on the basis of the general population and housing census data of 2011 and was used to prepare statistical information in 2010-2012.

Significant differences in entrepreneurship of urban and rural residents occur in Lithuania. Unexpected is that part of the self-employed quite significantly decreased (from 9.1 to 6.7 percent) in the city in 1998-2012. Although, job creation opportunities, in general, are much better in cities (especially in large cities) than in rural areas. Formally assessing, there are many more self-employed persons in rural areas than in urban areas (17.5 percent in 2012), but the latter jobs were created mainly in the agrarian sector. It shows a one-sided entrepreneurship orientation of rural population, but rate of the self-employed population declined from 34 to 17 percent in rural areas in 1998-2012 when employment in agriculture has decreased.

The situation in smaller regions of the country of self-employment (entrepreneurship) of the population of the country can be assessed in greater details using results from Lithuanian Real Estate Association survey which was carried out in 2012; the results were based on the State Social Insurance Fund Board data. This study showed a reduction of entrepreneurship opportunities of residents of smaller areas of the country during the economic crisis (Figure 1).

Figure 1. **Population Entrepreneurship Rate in 2009 and 2011***(percent of self-employed from the total population according to State Social Insurance Fund Board data)

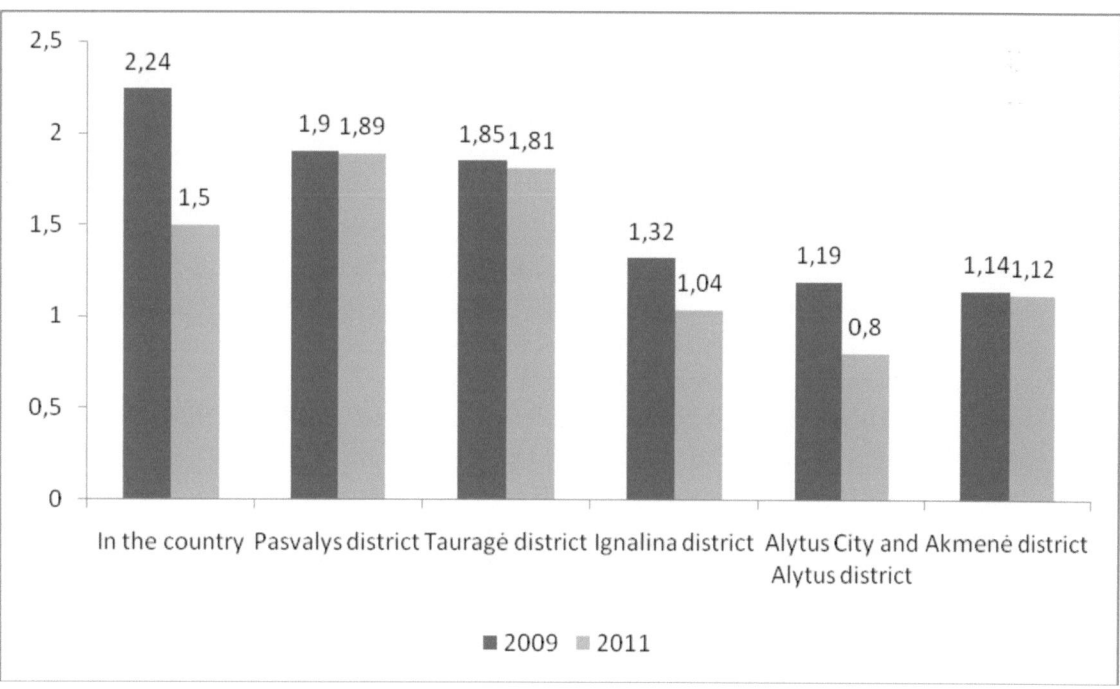

*Note: the rate of entrepreneurship that is presented in the chart does not include the farmers and their partners, and reflects the situation in the non-agricultural area. In addition, unlike the calculations carried out by Statistics Lithuania, the latter relative size was calculated by the study authors from the general population, rather than from the rate of the employed, therefore, its values are significantly lower than the ones in the previously accomplished analysis.

Lithuanian Real Estate Association survey showed that especially large portion of insured employed consists of hired employees. This already indirectly evidences of their poor extent of the organization of business opportunities in the regions of the country. Entrepreneurship rate, which in this case expresses the part of self-employed (people having their own busines) among the total population according to the analyzed territories, was extremely low (was only 1-2 percent) in 2009. This indicator was slightly higher in 2009 country wide; although the economic situation gradually stabilized later, the values of this index still were slightly lower in 2011 (ranged from 0.8 to 1.9 percent in regional level).

The possibilities of entrepreneurship in Lithuania will be briefly examined in terms of demographics. Women take to set up businesses and create enterprises by a long way less frequently than men in Europe. The latter feature is confirmed by the analysis of the situation in Lithuania. According to Statistics Lithuania, 599 thousand women worked wage labour in 2012 (men – 535 thousand). Hired women were almost 65 thousand more than men. About 50 thousand self-employed women were in 2012, whereas men were by a long way more – 75 thousand (Table 2). Unfortunately, the latter official indicators cannot tell anything about opportunities of the different demographic and social groups to better assess business risks, anticipate trends and prospects. But the available statistics already suggest about the fact that women are more likely to work for hire than men, and there are more men among the self-employed persons (the creation of one's own business usually requires more risk).

Table 2. **Employed persons by employment status in Lithuania in 2012**
(data from Statistics Lithuania)

	Total (in thousands)	Men (in thousands)	Women (in thousands)	Total (%)	Men (%)	Women (%)
In total	1275.7	617.6	658.1	100	100	100
Self-employed persons	124.3	75	49.2	9.7	12.1	7,5
Employees	1134.7	535.4	599.3	89.0	86.7	91,1
Contributing members of the family	16.7	7.1	9.6	1.3	1.2	1,4

The entrepreneurship of older people is relatively low in Lithuania judging from results of Lithuanian Enterpreneurship Observation survey which was carried out in 2012. Enterpreneurship of middle-aged and elderly people declined in 2011-2012. The proportion of older than 45 years people who have established their own business has fallen from 28 to 19 percent in this period. While it is difficult to assess whether the latter variation within a few years is not random, and to a large extent related with the possible influence of biases, but from data of this study it is evident that entrepreneurship of older people is considerably lower than of young people. Part of people aged over 45 years old was only 19 percent among those who have established their own business in 2012, whereas younger people under 35 years old were even about 60 percent.[15]

Judging from the statistics, job creation opportunities in autonomous business in the Baltic countries were worse than the EU average (Figure 2). Share of the self-employed was about 10 percent of the total number of the employed in Lithuania and Latvia, this rate was slightly lower in Estonia. However, observed trends are the most adverse in Lithuania. Part of the self-employed in Lithuania declined during the period of 2005-2012, nevertheless, this rate increased slightly in other Baltic countries. Women's self-employment opportunities were lower than men's. Proportion of persons with their own business among employed women was only 7.3 percent in Lithuania, 8.1 percent in Latvia, and 4.6 percent in Estonia in 2012. During the longer period of time, changes of self-employment were not favourable in the whole EU. A part of employed people in their own business decreased from 14.9 to 14.5 percent in 2005-2012. However, this negative change was relatively small. A similar trend is observed in old states of EU. Self-employed share in the total employment decreased from 14.4 to 14.2 percent during this period in the EU-15 countries.

In order to control the impact of demographic change and promote innovation-based economy, it is important to promote the economic activity and employment of different groups of the population, and to develop socially responsible business. The study, which was carried out by Swedbank in 2013, shows that men more actively establish the new companies in the Baltic countries and Sweden. In Lithuania, Latvia, Estonia and Sweden, business, which is established by women, accounts for almost one third of all new businesses created, businesses, which are established by men, account for more than two-thirds.Thus, women establish their own businesses twice rarely than men in the Baltic countries and Sweden. 30-40 years old residents mostly take business, while increased

---

[15]Laužikas M., Vaiginienė E. ir kiti. Lietuvos verslumo stebėsenos tyrimo rezultatai (studija). Vilnius (2012).

entrepreneurship rate of especially young people is noticeable in Lithuania. It is also noted that after the recession, since 2011, the number of older than 50 years old men, who are establishing business, decreased, while the number of women of the same age, who are establishing their own business, has remained almost unchanged. According to Swedbank's Small Business Services Department director Jurgita Blazgienė, Lithuania complies with EU trends, and though in Lithuania more women than men have university education, women's entrepreneurship is still lower.

Figure 2. **Percentage of Self-employed** (Eurostat data, %)*

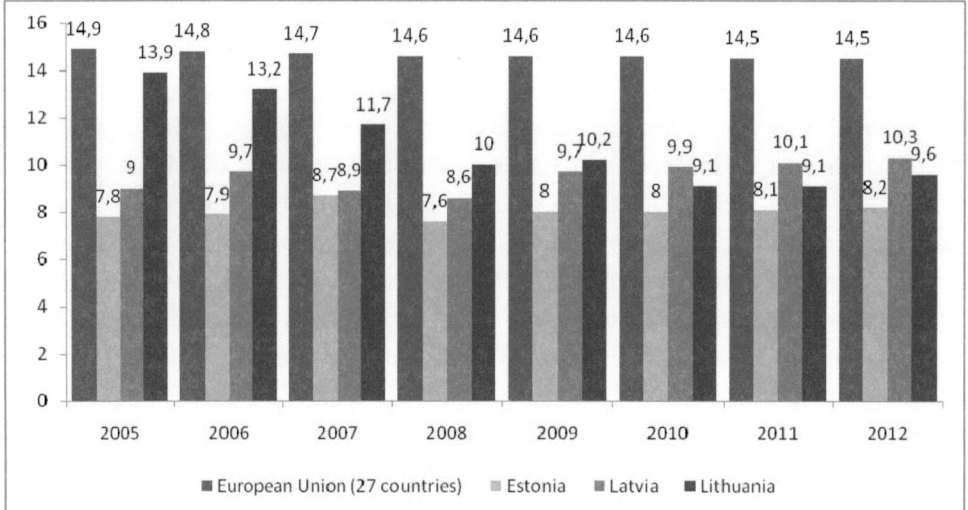

*15-64 years old population employment rate.

According to Eurostat, men also dominated among business managers in Lithuania in 2011. 11.6 percent men who participate in the labour market took the head position, while managing women accounted for 6.9 percent. The female gender dominates in groups of experts, service sector workers and saleswomen.This suggests that in Lithuania women try to take less risk in group of managing professions and prefer jobs of specialists and hired employees.

In addition, men and women establish business in different areas. According to Swedbank, in Lithuania women more often establish the sewing, beauty and health care enterprises, small restaurants and cafes, hotels, sports clubs, odontology and private

44

treatment consulting-rooms. And in neighbouring Latvia, the most popular companies that were established by women operate in areas of accounting, auditing and tax consulting. Women are also establishing retail, food service, beauty care, real estate management, clothing and textile retail, rummage and transport companies. In Estonia entrepreneurship tendencies of women are similar to Lithuania's and Latvia's – women establish one third of all businesses. However, according to J. Blazgienė, this country is distinguished for number of women managers in businesses which are traditionally non-feminine: the ratio of women and men holding management positions in those businesses is much more favourable in Estonia than in Lithuania and Latvia.[16]

Labour Market Flexibility

Labour market flexibility is most often associated with the liberalization of labour relations and the reduction of the state's role in the labour market. Guarantees of employment are developed through employment security measures, implementing social insurance and social dialogue principles, through active labour market policies and its measures, which help workers to adapt to changes in the labour market and promote professional mobility. As stated in the official documents of the European Commission, guarantees of flexibility are related to successful transition from one stage of life to another: from school to work, from one job to another, from period of unemployment to work, and from work to retirement. They are not related entirely with more freedom for companies to engage and stand off persons, and they do not mean that open-ended contracts are obsolete. They are related to the pursuit of better job, the opportunities to pursue higher positions and the best spread of talent. Guarantees of flexibility are related to flexible work organization, when there is the ability to quickly and effectively adapt to new production requirements and to acquire new skills, they are also related to easier harmonization of vocational and personal responsibilities.[17] However, labour market flexibility is excessively counterposed against employment security in labour market policy area, though their balance is declared.

---

[16]Swedbank, AB. In the Baltic Countries and Sweden, Women Establish Their Own Businesses Twice More Rarely than Men. Available at: <http://www.swedbank.lt/lt/articles/view/1782>.

[17]*With the View of the Common Principles of Flexicurity, Combining Guarantees of Flexibility and Employment to Create More and Better Jobs.* Communication from the Commission to the European Parliament, the Council, the European Economic and Social Committee and the Committee of the Regions. {SEK(2007) 861}, KOM(2007) 359 final. Brussels (2007).

People say that the balance of the flexibility of the labour market and guarantees of employment is a political approach which seeks to combine labour market flexibility concerning employers and employment guarantees of workers.[18] However, this conception of labour market flexibility is possible from the approach that the flexibility reflects only the employer's interests. It is accepted that the employer and employee relationship should be based on an equality bases, already flexible labour market itself should reflect the balance of coordination of the interests of its different participants, while its own flexibility would not be coordinated only with the interests of business (especially large) resprematives; justification of implementing those interests was so fiercely advocated by ideologues of free market (especially in Eastern European countries).

It is believed that it is necessary to change the conceptual approach to that very conception of labour market flexibility. The very flexibility of the labour market should be based on namely through CSR. CSR is a way to ensure labour market flexibility combining employer and amployee interests. Promoting CSR, each EU country could ensure a flexible working of their labour markets through the optimal balance of interests allowing this to reflect opportunities of employment guarantees application in the labour market policy. The scientific literature suggests that labour market flexibility and employment security concept providing more questions than answers, nevertheless, should be systematically analyzed in relation to the labour market, social security and economic policy issues.[19] The attitude is expressed that the flexicurity concept is not viable if flexibility is associated only with the needs of employers, and security – with the needs of employees.[20]

Temporary employment opportunities reflect labour market flexibility. However, it should be more not a replacement form of employment, which would be applied by force instead of full-time employment, but a measure of the inclusion of additional employment resources into the labour market. The proportion of temporary employed persons among

---

[18]*The Balance of Labour Market Flexibility and Guarantees of Employment – Issues and Tasks.*European Foundation for the Improvement of Living and Working Conditions (2009).
[19]Skučienė D., Moskvina J.*Saugumas lanksčioje darbo rinkoje.* Social Work. Scientific Works. Vilnius: Mykolas Romeris University (2008. No. 7(1)).
[20]Wilthagen, T. Flexicurity: *A New Paradigm for Labour Market Policy Reform?* Discussion Paper FS II 98-02,
Wissenschaftszentrum fur Sozialforschung. Berlin (1998).

all hired employees is significantly higher in EU than in the Baltic countries (Figure 3).This indicator has increased only in Estonia in 1998-2012, whereas in the other Baltic countries it has decreased significantly despite significant fluctuations. This indicator decreased particularly in Lithuania (from 6.5 to 2.6 percent). Traditionally, this indicator remained the highest among the Baltic countries in Latvia (4.8 percent in 2012). Temporary jobs were created relatively slightly more for women than for men in EU (the proportion of women who were temporarily employed on the average amounted to 14.2 percent in EU in 2012 and exceeded the overall average of this index), but the relative opportunities of establishment of temporary jobs for women in the Baltic countries were lower than for men. In 2012, proportion of women who were temporarily employed was only 1.9 percent in Lithuania, 2.5 percent in Estonia, 3.3 percent in Latvia, and proportion of men who were temporarily employed was 3.5 percent in Lithuania, 4.6 percent in Estonia, and 6.3 percent in Latvia.

Figure 3. **Temporary Employees as Percentage of the Total Number of Employees** (Eurostat data, %)

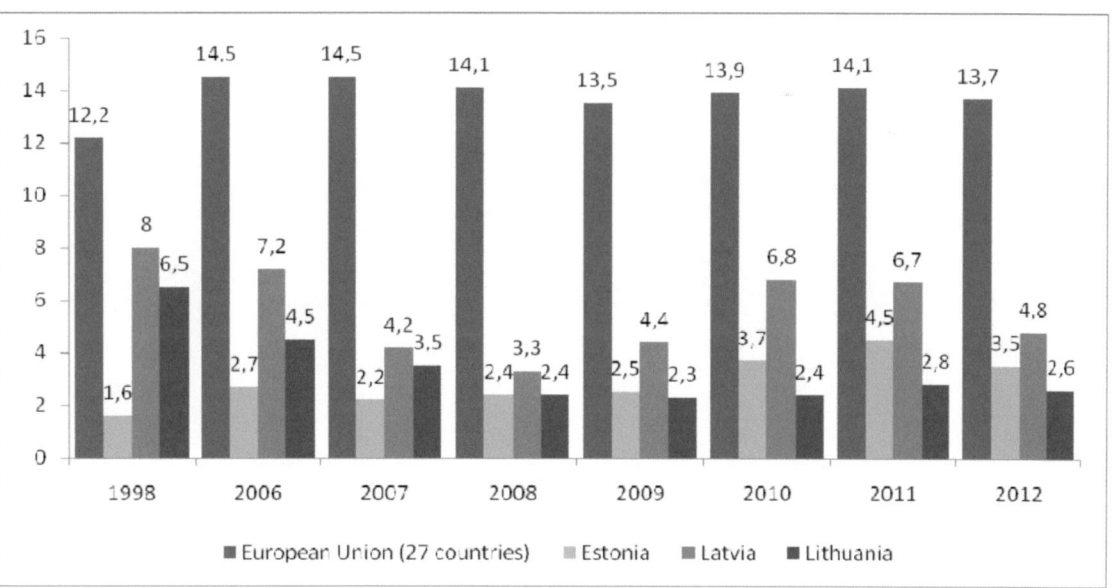

Note: Rate of EU-27 is given since 2000 (data from 1998 is not available).

Part-time work is another perhaps the most popular flexible form of employment. Despite the significant temporal variations, part of the employed part-time has increased slightly (from 8.5 to 8.8 percent) in Lithuania in 1998-2012, a positive change, which is observed in Estonia, was more significant (from 6.7 to 9.2 percent), whereas this rate decreased from 11.7 to 8.9 percent in Latvia. At the beginning of the observed period, Latvia was leader in accordance with the meaning of this index, whereas at the end of the last decade, Estonia made a push into the first place, but in general, assimilation trend of index values of the employment of part-time was observed. Approximately every tenth woman, who worked in Latvia and Lithuania, used this flexible form of employment during the last three four years, while rate of women's employment of part-time increased to 13 percent during this decade in Estonia (Fig. 4).

Figure 4. **Part-time Employment as Percentage of the Total Employment**
(Eurostat data, %)

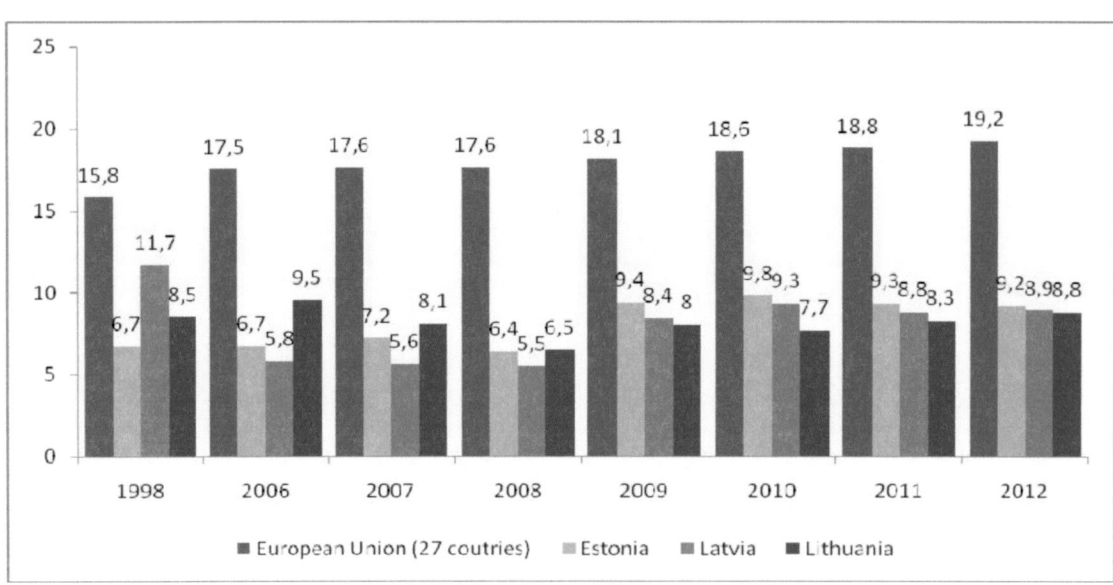

Note: Rate of EU-27 is given since 2000 (data from 1998 is not available).

Studies and scientists' remarks suggest that high level of flexibility, employment, social security or income guarantees is not essentially typical of the Lithuanian labour market.[21] In other words, Lithuania is not also characterized by high flexibility or high security.[22] For example, according to the wage structure research data, Lithuania, Latvia, and Macedonia have the highest part of workers who get low wages. In 2010, this relative indicator amounted to 27 percent in Lithuania and 28 percent in Latvia and Macedonia. This indicator amounted to 26 percent in Romania. Statistical data show that distribution of the structure of earnings is very unfavourable for workers in these countries. The relative weight of workers who receive low wages was significantly lower in other EU countries (Fig. 5).

Figure 5 (next page). **Proportion of a Low Wage Recipients of the Country's Total Employed Population (Excluding Trainees)** (Eurostat data) (wage structure survey) (percent)

[21]Gruževskis B., Blažienė I.*Lankstumas ir saugumas darbo rinkoje. Lietuvos patirtis.* Flexicurity paper 2004/5. Budapest: International Labour Office (2005).
[22]Tangian, A. *Flexicurity: Is Employment Security Attainable under Flexible Employment? Empirical Evidence, Critical Remarks, and Reform Proposal.* Paper for the conference of the Portugal Presidency in the EU "Flexicurity: Key Challenges". Lisbon (September 13–14, 2007).

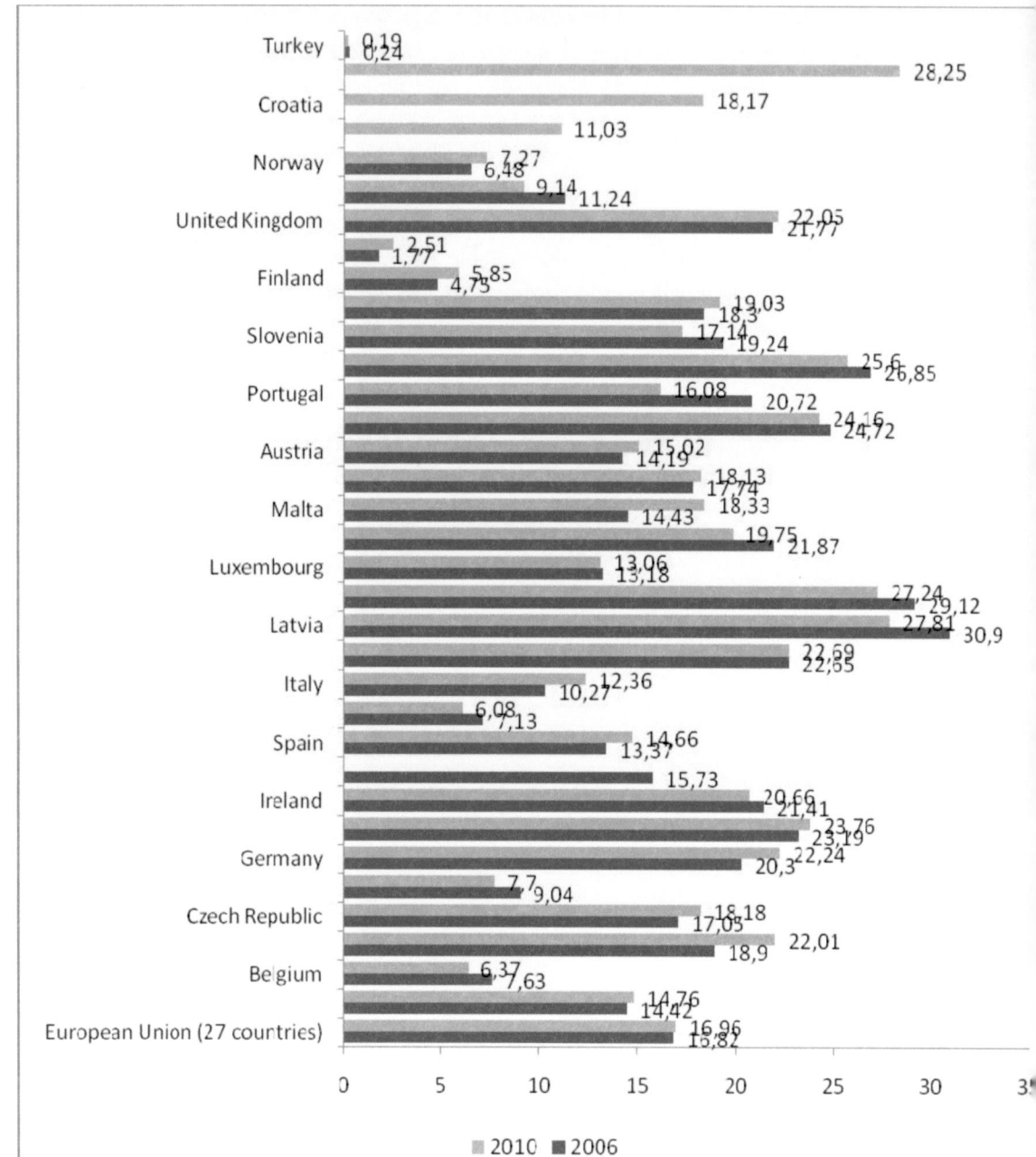

*The study includes wage assessment of employees employed in companies of 10 or more employees.

Note: the study was not carried out in the individual countries in a particular year.

The more jobs are created, the more vibrant and flexible labour market is. The companies of the country in one way or another promote to the development of CSR (especially under favourable conditions for business development) by creating new jobs. But even more importantly, in terms of the development of CSR is that the newly created jobs would be attractive and would provide an adequate standard of living for employees of companies and for their families. Therefore, sustainable business growth opportunities are particularly important in the formation of favourable conditions for the development of CSR.

Although the overall rate of openings gradually began to grow again after the shock during the economic crisis in Lithuania, but in 2012 it was almost two times lower than in 2008 (Figure 6). This reflects the substantial long-term consequences of the economic crisis on the labour market. Jobs were especially "cropped" in the financial and insurance activities, and in construction. Nearly least negative openings change was felt in trade and stuff repair, where the openings rate was 1.1 percent in 2008 and 0.9 percent in 2012.

Figure 6. **The Dynamics of Openings Level in Lithuania According to the Main Economic Activities** (Statistics Lithuania data) (in percent)

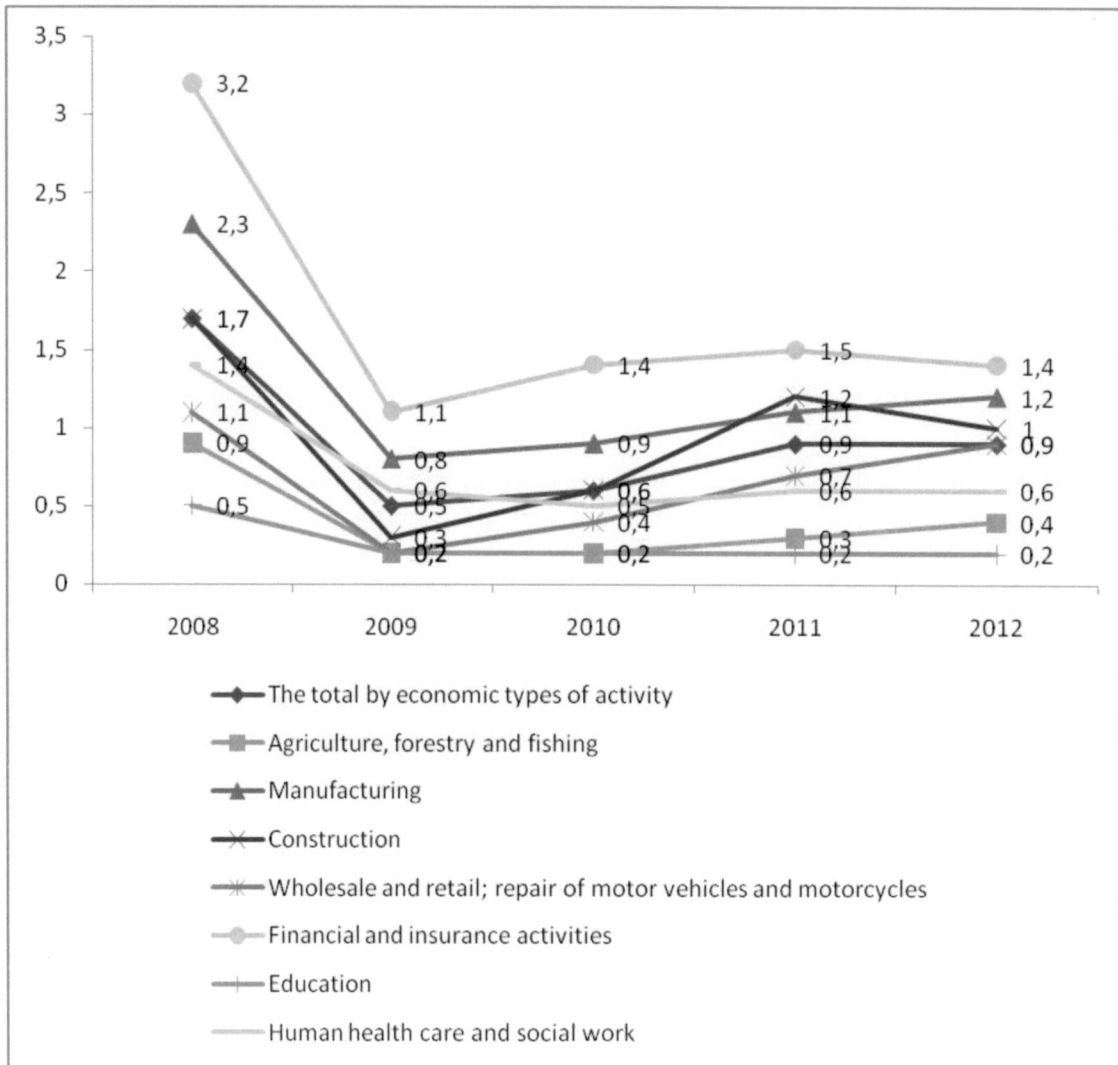

Conclusion

The traditions of CSR are formed and developed in Lithuania using the experience of the EU and various international organizations. Various factors interact with each other and influence opportunities of CSR promotion and development. Former economic crisis has had a serious injury to the development of CSR. Many companies in the country in 2008-2010 reduced staff salaries and unemployment significantly increased. It is therefore very important that the CSR principles would be implemented also in difficult business conditions, not just declared. Recovery of the national economy created favorable conditions for the development of a new CSR pulse. Various companies and institutions should make better use of arising opportunities for CSR development.

Job creation opportunities depend on the level of entrepreneurship. Successful socially responsible development of own business makes it easier for creating attractive jobs. However, the statistical analysis of the data shows that the entrepreneurship of the population of the country (especially women) is rather low. This shows that actually in Lithuania the reserves of entrepreneurship is not used in sector of small business.

As we can see from the publication material, there are many factors in Lithuania that both encourage and stop CSR. It can be said that CSR and its options depend on the these factors and interactions. Objective knowledge about their impact on the development of CSR is very lacking. Therefore, CSR development opportunities and assessment of the factors influencing it requires significantly more education and other institutions to broader investigations.

Different researchers observe that high level of flexibility, employment, social security and guarantees of income is not generally typical of Lithuanian labour market. More flexible and influenced by the traditions of the development of CSR, the labour market would help to better deal with the working integration problems of women and other social groups of the population. Experience shows that women's opportunities to employ for part-time job significantly determine the increase of women's employment. However, these opportunities are poorly exploited in Lithuania and other Baltic countries. Almost one third of women worked half-day in Europe at the beginning of this decade, whereas only one tenth such women were in Lithuania and Latvia, such women were slightly more in Estonia (13 percent). It is believed that half-day should not be forced replacement of full population employment. This is a form of employment, which should encourage inactive women and older people to enter the labour market at the same time increasing the activity of the population and their opportunities to participate in the labour market.

Relative opportunities of temporary job creation were much lower in the Baltic countries than on the average in EU. In 2012, temporary work accounted for only 2.6 percent of the total number of hired employees in Lithuania, values of this index were slightly higher in the other Baltic countries (EU-27 average was 13.7 percent). On the other hand, a little more temporary jobs are created for women than for men in EU (accordingly 14.2 and 13.2 percent).

Analysis of the data shows that Lithuanian companies relatively seldom use flexible forms of employment for placement of job seekers. Therefore, one of the directions of development of CSR in the country would be broader application of flexible forms of employment by helping unemployed people to more successfully integrate into the labour market. In particular, it concerns women with minor children and persons with disabilities engaging them for part-time working. Application of flexible forms of employment for the elderly would help to increase their opportunities to participate in the labour market by extending their period of activity. In other words, the wider application of flexible forms of employment would enable to better use potential opportunities of existing labour resources (particularly more skilled people).

Attitudes of employers themselves (i.e. attitude towars their application) greatly influence limited application of flexible forms of employment in Lithuania. However, those factors that are largely dependent on the behaviour of workers in the labour market should largely influence the choice of the usual form of employment instead of flexible forms of employment in the country.It is believed that a large part of the jobseekers gives a priority to work full time only because the latter form of employment better reflects the aspirations of workers to secure their own and their families in meeting the needs which usually could not be guaranteed by work half-day or temporary employment in case of low wage. Thus, a limited application of flexible forms of employment in the country should be associated with the traditions of low wages.On the other hand, small opportunities of options of attractive jobs in the country's businesses should encourage the provision of workers to choose traditional forms of employment.

Under present conditions, one's own business could become one of the more significant sources of growth of population activity and increase in interest of working in acceptable material conditions, when opportunities of jobs in a large extent are already exhausted in the largest companies. This is one way to help get rid of "country of cheap labour force" epithet for Lithuania. It is rather difficult to talk about socially responsible small business in the country, when self-employment of residents declined for a long time. It can be said that there was obviously a lack of measures which would operate effectively and promote small business in Lithuania.On the other hand, a particular small gleam appeared in this decade: self-employment of the population gradually began to grow in this decade, although it is difficult to assess how long this favourable trend can last.

List of References

Academic Publications and Studies

1. *Bendros socialinės atsakomybės tendencijos tarp mažų ir vidutinių įmonių Baltijos šalyse* (tyrimą atliko verslo konsultacijų įmonė "EKT grupė", Lietuvoje įgyvendinusi Europos Komisijos iš dalies finansuojamą projektą) (2007 m. balandis).

2. *Corporate Social Responsibility National public policies in the European Union* (07/05/2008). Prieiga per internetą: http://ec.europa.eu/social/main.jsp?catId=331&langId=en&pubId=61&type=2&furtherPubs=yes.

3. *Darbo rinkos lankstumo ir užimtumo garantijų pusiausvyra – problemos ir uždaviniai.* Europos gyvenimo ir darbo sąlygų gerinimo fondas (2009).

4. Ehaab A. Nelson J., Fahmy A., Greenwald D. *The Status and Potential of Social Entrepreneurship in the Middle East. Brookings Institution* (April 27, 2010).

5. Forstater M., Zadek S, Guang Y, Yu K., Xiao C., George H.M. *Corporate Resposibility in African Development Insigrhts from an Emergening Dialog.* CSRI Working Paper No. 60 (October 2010).

6. Gruževskis B., Blažienė I. *Lankstumas ir saugumas darbo rinkoje. Lietuvos patirtis.* Flexicurity paper 2004/5. Budapeštas: Tarptautinis darbo biuras (2005).

7. Laužikas M., Vaiginienė E ir kiti. *Lietuvos verslumo stebėsenos tyrimo rezultatai (studija).* Vilnius (2012).

8. Rees C., Kemp D, and Davis R. *Conflict Management and Corporate Culture in the Extractives Sector: A Study in Peru.* CSRI Report No. 50. (September, 2012).

9. Skučienė D., Moskvina J. *Saugumas lanksčioje darbo rinkoje.* Socialinis darbas. Mokslo darbai. Vilnius: Mykolo Romerio univeristetas (2008. Nr. 7(1)).

10. Tangian, A. *Flexicurity: Is Employment Security Attainable under Flexible Employment? Empirical Evidence, Critical Remarks, and Reform Proposal.* Paper for the conference of the Portugal Presidency in the EU "Flexicurity: Key Challenges". Lisbon (September 13–14, 2007).

11. *Verslo plėtra Lietuvoje ir Vidurio Europoje.* Vilnius: LR Ūkio ministerija, Statistikos departamentas (2000).

12. Wilthagen, T. Flexicurity: *A New Paradigm for Labour Market Policy Reform?* Discussion Paper FS II 98-02, Wissenschaftszentrum fur Sozialforschung Berlin (1998).

13. Žukauskas R. S. *Smulkaus ir vidutinio verslo plėtros strateginės kryptys.* Viešoji politika ir administravimas. Vilnius (2002, Nr. 1).

Other Sources of Information

14. Europos komisija (http://ec.europa.eu/social/main.jsp?catId=331&langId=lt).

15. Įmonių socialinės atsakomybės plėtros 2009-2013 m. programa ir jos įgyvendinimo 2009–2011 metų priemonių planas (Vilnius, 2010 m. sausio 12 d.). Prieiga per internetą:
    http://www3.lrs.lt/pls/inter3/dokpaieska.showdoc_l?p_id=363948&p_query=&p_tr 2=.

16. Siekiant bendrų lankstumo ir užimtumo garantijų principų: derinant lankstumo ir užimtumo garantijas kurti daugiau ir geresnių darbo vietų. Komisijos komunikatas Europos Parlamentui, Tarybai, Europos ekonomikos ir socialinių reikalų komitetui ir Regionų komitetui. SEK (2007) 861}, KOM (2007) 359 galutinis. Briuselis (2007).

17. Socialinės apsaugos ir darbo ministerija (http://www.socmin.lt).

18. Tyrimas: Lietuvoje socialinė sanglauda silpna. Prieiga per internetą: http://m.alfa.lt/naujienos/Lietuva/28470/

19. http://vkc.vtf.lt/apieĮSA.

20. http://europa.eu/legislation_summaries/employment_and_social_policy/job_creatio n_measures/index_lt.htm.

21. AB „Swedbank". Baltijos šalyse ir Švedijoje moterys nuosavą verslą kuria dvigubai rečiau nei vyrai. Prieiga per internetą: http://www.swedbank.lt/lt/articles/view/1782.

22. http://europa.eu/youreurope/business/environment/energy-labels/index_lt.htm#lithuania_lt_taking-sustainability-further.

23. http://europa.eu/legislation_summaries/employment_and_social_policy/job_creat ion_measures/index_lt.htm.http://www.socmin.lt/index.php?1822387092

24. http://www.socmin.lt/index.php?-2084770119.

The Analysis of the situation of vulnerable population groups in Lithuanian Labour Market, Review of research

Laima Okunevičiūtė-Neverauskienė

Vilnius Gediminas Technical University, Faculty of Business Management, Social Economy and Business Management Department

Julija Moskvina

Institute of Labour and Social Research of Lithuanian Social Research Centre

According to a secondary analysis of statistical data and specialized researches data, it is pursued to review the situation of different target groups in the labour market in the context of shifting economic challenges. The situation of men and women, youth and older, as well as disabled people in Lithuanian labour market is examined in this article. The aim is to reveal the factors that determine the integration of the vulnerable population groups into the labour market, thus, it is outlined how the different level implementers of social and employment policy most effectively contribute to these processes of integration. Studies are also used in the publication; the main objective of these studies is not directly related to the topic of vulnerable people position in the labour market, but the results are significant taking into account the specifics of the different population groups.

Keywords: labour market groups at risk, women, disabled people, youth, elderly people.

Introduction

Problems and possibilities of vulnerable persons in the labour market have been studied fairly extensively in Lithuania during the last decade. The growing number of studies of the situation of different risk groups in the labour market is indirectly associated with Lithuania's accession to the EU and the country's assumed obligations to contribute to the implementation of objectives of the European Employment Strategy. Projects or evaluation studies of other social initiatives make quite a large part of researches that were done in the country; especially the EQUAL initiative in Lithuania should be mentioned; the projects are funded from the European Social Fund. The responsible authorities also initiated the accomplishment of researches while planning or evaluating changes in policy of population social security and employment.

The aim of this article is to review the situation of women, the disabled, youth and the elderly in the labour market in the context of changing economic challenges according to a secondary analysis of statistical data and specialized researches data.

Typically, researchers who are interested in the topic of vulnerable groups in the labour market distinguish these target groups of the population: women, youth, old-timers, the long-term unemployed (Matiušaitytė, 2001), as well as more specific groups of unemployed people – the elderly, the disabled, non-basic education (Gruževskis et al., 2006b). Despite the fact that Lithuania lacks the complex, sequential researches, as well as detailed statistical data reflecting the situation of different vulnerable persons and the dynamics in the labour market, review of researches enables to define the primary barriers for the integration of isolated target groups into employment.

Fluctuations in the economic cycles inevitably have an impact on population employment trends, more detailed analysis of employment and unemployment rates according to various groups of the population shows their different possibilities of adaptation to changing labour market conditions. The recent economic crisis has highlighted the issues of the involvement of young people into professional life, as well as the issues of the quality of their employment. Such problems of the integration of disabled people into employment as professional preparation of disabled youth and re-integration of working age people with disabilities into the labour market are waiting for more effective decisions. Unfavourable demographic trends, increasingly cumulative imbalances of labour supply and demand in the country show the need of measures which were pointed to elongation of productive working age.

Situation of Women and Men in the Labour Market

In Lithuania, in comparison with other European countries, women's participation in the labour market is high. Women's Information Centre survey that was carried out in 2009 showed that women's provisions for participation in the labour market become even stronger: women and men preferred men's employment until 1994 (inclusive) on condition that there was the lack of jobs in the labour market. Majority of women already disapproved of this provision in 2000, and the accord of the population of Lithuania disapproved of this provision in 2009. 70 percent Lithuanian population chooses family, where husband and wife work and both take care of home and children (Women and Men in the Society of Lithuania, 2009).

The assessment of employment by gender reveals that the male employment rate has traditionally been higher than that of women. It was especially high among men before the economic crises in 1998 and 2007 (amounted to almost 60 percent). However, the male employment rate declined rapidly when unfavourable economic conditions were evidenced.

The dynamics of unemployment and employment indicators allowed to see that the effects of the economic downturn on the various economic sectors and on people employed in those sectors are different. Hired employees who had low qualification and worked in industry and construction sectors were the worst affected during the crisis in 2008. More rapidly changing number of unemployed men is one of the most striking consequences which were conditioned by economic fluctuations and structural changes in the economy. Fluctuations of women's employment rate were much lower during the change of economic conditions. Women's employment rate decreased from 48.9 to 46 percent during the period of 2007-2010 and was felt significantly less than equivalent change of men's ratio.

Figure 1. **Employment and Unemployment Rates by Gender** (%)

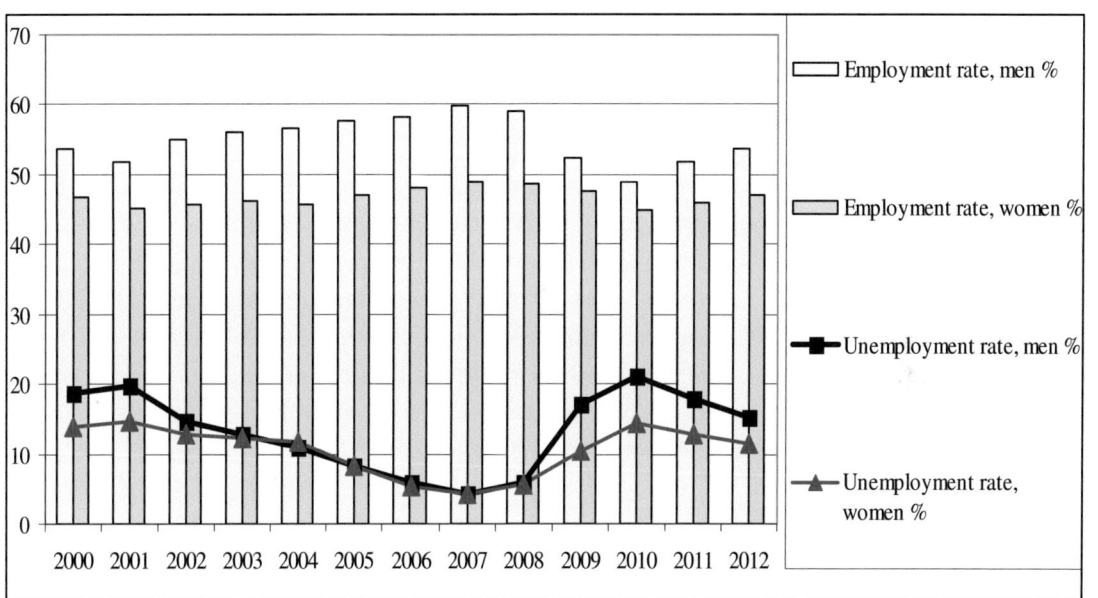

Source: Statistics Lithuania.

A group of unemployed men more quickly than women have adapted and returned to employment due to changes in the situation in the labour market. The analysis of Lithuanian employment and unemployment rates by gender confirms that it is more difficult for women to move from unemployment to employment when labour market conditions change in the favourable way during the post-crisis period. For example, analysis of the structure of the unemployed by gender shows a lower flexibility of female employment with regard to economic fluctuations – the proportions of the long-term unemployed decrease more slowly in the group of women.

The horizontal segregation of the labour market has remained virtually of the same level, or even worse; it was observed during the analysis of the last decade women's and men's employment trends by economic types of activity. Human health care and social work, activities of accommodation and food service, as well as education remained the main field of activity of women. Women represented major part among junior specialists and technicians, junior officers and service and sales workers. Women also amount to 67 percent public sector employees (*Statistics Lithuania. Employed and Hired*). The textile industry, health care and education remain women's "traditional" spheres of employment. In addition, more women than men have lower incomes, thus, a threat of the feminisation of poverty remains in Lithuania (Women and Men in the Society of Lithuania, 2009).

Studies show that unemployment affects men and women differently. First of all, it should be noted that sectors of the economy that require men's labour force experience the largest decline during the economic downturn, thus, the unemployment rate of men is growing much faster than that of women. Accordingly, unemployed men more quickly find a job during the recovery of the national economy. Secondly, the unemployed men and women have different opportunities to anchor in the labour market. There is a major chance for unemployed women to stay out of work for a long time (longer than 12 months). Thirdly, women who are victims of long-term unemployment more hardly return to the labour market.

The differences of women's and men's transition from employment to unemployment and from unemployment to employment demonstrate that the population group of men in the labour market is more flexible, while the adaptation of a group of women to changes in the labour market is slower, therefore, the macroeconomic processes can have long-term negative consequences. It can be assumed that women are more interested in preserving their jobs, and it leads to the choice of the profession and the preferred form of the employment. In this case, the salary may play a less important role in women's choice of job than in men's.

People with Disabilities

The new *Law on Social Integration of the Disabled* came into force in Lithuania on the 1st of July in 2005 (Official Gazette, 2004, No. 83-2983); this law brought a lot of innovations and changes in the concept of disability, the assessment criteria, the order of determination, and the system of the disabled social security guarantees. A transitional period of 2 years from the "old" (disablement) system to the "new" (disability and working capacity level) systems was provided in this law and this period ended on the 1st of July in 2007. It is concluded that the reform laid the foundations for formation of a genuine integrative policy for the disabled, when the analysis of the changes in the determination of disability and the appointment of related benefits during the reform (Žalimienė et al., 2007); this is typical of most other EU countries.

The reform means that Lithuania is expanding assistance to the disabled. In addition to pensions, this aid covers professional rehabilitation, job search assistance, supported employment, job application and provision of technical assistance means, etc. The directions of the reform are reasonable, because the needs of people with disabilities are not limited to material guarantees and pension.

Rejection of disability term in Lithuanian social law is very important in order to reduce stigmatization and discrimination against people with disabilities. However, entrenchment of the terms "disability", "lost working capacity" may adversely affect the integration of disabled persons into the labour market. This raises the question how to argue equal treatment of disabled people, when they enter into the labour market, if they have "lost working capacity". Since the integration of disabled persons into the labour market is highly dependent not only on the person's functionality, capacity to work, but also on the stereotypes, it is important to change the terms and usable rhetoric.

The following facts were noted during the analysis of the labour market of people with disabilities in the supply aspect (Skučienė, Šumskaitė, 2005): the working-age people with disabilities amount to only slightly more than half of the total number of the disabled; severely disabled persons account for about one tenth of all persons with disabilities; two thirds of people with disabilities live in urban areas; the unemployment rate of people with disabilities is higher in rural areas; a large proportion of working-age people with disabilities is unskilled; a quarter of disabled people does not have professional preparation; even one tenth of disabled people has no education (the findings were presented on the basis of Population Census data (2001) and Ministry of Social Security and Labour, Statistics Lithuania, Lithuanian Labour Exchange data (2004)).

"Labour Market Policy Measures Influence on Employment in Different Conditions of Cycle of Economic Development" survey, which was carried out by Labour and Social Research Institute in 2011-2013, also reveals the unfavourable trends of persons with disabilities employment. According to the State Social Insurance Fund Board, almost 47 thousand persons with disabilities in total worked in the country at the beginning of 2012 (Table 1). During the analysis of the number of recipients of disability (invalidity) pensions and disabled employees, it is noticed that every five working-age disabled is working in the country (21 percent). The pre-crisis period and the post-crisis period were compared; the proportion of working disability pensioners in total number of recipients of disability (invalidity) pensions declined slightly – only 3 percent (from 22 percent at the beginning of 2009 to 19 percent at the beginning of 2010).

During the analysis of the dynamics of employed persons with disabilities, it is noted that the number of the employed disability pensioners rapidly grew till the end of 2008, while it fell by about 8 percent during the crisis (from 48 thousand till 44 thousand). Despite the economic downturn, the participation of persons with disabilities in the labour market started to grow again and the number of disabled employees has exceeded the index of the end of 2007 at the end of 2011.

Table 1.**Working Lost Working Capacity Pensioners** (total under disability, at the beginning of the period)

2005	2006	2007	2008	2009	2010	2011	2012
30572	33612	37940	44811	48252	44434	44886	46666

The highest weight among the recipients of state social insurance lost working capacity pensions comes to persons who have average disability (60-70 percent). Nearly three out of five employed persons with disabilities have 60-70 percent lost working capacity level. 35 percent employed people with disabilities have easier disability (45-55 percent lost working capacity level). One out of ten employed disabled has severe disability – 75-100 percent lost working capacity level.

Data that were received again revealed previously observed trend: major disability and lower (0-40 percent) working capacity level, which is related to it, remain a serious barrier for these people to integrate into the labour market. Disabled persons of higher (40-55 percent) working capacity level establish themselves easier in the labour market. Judging from the results of the research (Okunevičiūtė-Neverauskienė et al., 2008), individuals of the lower working capacity level are much more passive in participation in the means of the labour exchange. However, ALMP measures help to retain links with the labour market and society for people who have started to participate in those measures. The involvement of project actors in measure certainly improved their psychological state and gave self-reliance. The study showed that the employers who are participating in the means began much better assess disabled workers; former sceptical attitude of employers towards the employment of people with disabilities began to wane.

This fact suggests that such projects contribute to the anti-discrimination provisions in regard to the disabled persons. An important condition for the successful employment of the disabled is application of flexible forms of employment in engaging participants of the project at half-day.

According to the Lithuanian Labour Exchange data, the disabled unemployed employ far more difficult if compared with those who do not have disability: the disabled unemployed who employed accounted for just 2 percent out of the total number of employed registered unemployed (the proportion of persons with disabilities in the total number of registered unemployed was 5.4 percent in 2006).

Indicators of participation of disabled people in vocational training and retraining programs do not represent high activity of this population group. Women with disabilities are involved more actively than disabled men in vocational training and retraining measures (women were about two-thirds of the participants); in addition, the participation of women remains relatively constant for many years, while the participation of men is changing. Women are more active visitors of day-care centres (DC) than men, although the number of both grows in activities of DC.

The extents of social services for disabled (provision of compensatory techniques, sign language translation, housing and environmental applications) continue to grow, although they are still quite in a low level; those social services could serve as an additional tool to increase employment. Rural residents with disabilities have fewer of these services than urban residents with disabilities.

People with disabilities themselves (Skučienė, Šumskaitė, 2005) identify the following key barriers to participate in the labour market: physical health status, negative opinion of employers to people with disabilities and low wages. They are also unhappy about the lack of attention of the labour exchange to employment of people with disabilities, limited mobility of persons with disabilities and environment which is not intended for their needs. The results of the survey for disabled showed that the following measures would help to ensure major participation of people with disabilities in the labour market: the application of more flexible forms or work organization and the rendering of larger opportunities for qualification improvement. Every tenth questioned disabled faces with job application problem. There are barriers to people with disabilities to develop business: not enough information to start their own business, low level of professional preparation of the disabled population, the lack of professional knowledge for business development, the lack of initial capital to start business, etc.

The qualitative research of employment of people with disabilities and education opportunities in Lithuania was carried out in 2007 (Šėporaitytė, Tereškinas, 2007); this research largely confirmed the above aforesaid propositions. According to the opinion of study informants with disabilities, it is difficult for a disabled person to employ because of the unfitted environment, the negative attitude of employers and co-workers, the lack of motivation to work, constraints caused by disability and the inability to handle some of the work.

The same study (Šėporaitytė, Tereškinas, 2007) demonstrates not only the position of the disabled for employment opportunities. Consultants of the Business Development of the Disabled Communities and Labour Exchanges claimed during the interview that their own unwillingness to work is one of the biggest barriers for disabled people to employ; other barriers are long periods of unemployment, lack of work experience, limitations imposed by disability and the negative attitude of employers. The results showed that employment often depends on the type of disability, level of working capacity and labour restrictions.

People with disabilities are one of consistently investigated groups during the examination of measures of the active labour market policy (ALMP). The study was carried out in 2007 and it showed that despite pessimistic considered employment opportunities, the target group of people with disabilities after ALMP showed the best results of employment of all vulnerable groups who participated in the means (Okunevičiūtė-Neverauskienė et al., 2007a). Studies have also shown that participation of people with disabilities in ALMP measures has very high social and psychological effect on them, but these factors are not considered at all in the national labour market policy. In this context it can be said that the researches of labour market participants should not only serve the need of policy making bodies, but also to look for new solutions and to improve the awareness of efficiency evaluation of the measures implemented.

The above presented results can be added to these valuable observations for integration of the disabled into the labour market. The research of integration of persons with hearing disabilities into the labour market (Bikmanienė et al., 2007a) showed that the predominant difficulties are communication problems; people with hearing impairments face these difficulties in the labour market. Deficiency of the required preparation and lack of suitable jobs for the deaf are also important barriers for the integration of deaf people into the labour market.

Employers assess critically, often unfavourably the opportunities of integration of people with mental illness into the labour market. This shows that fear and distrust encourage stigma and discrimination of people with mental illness. The study identified the causes of unemployment which are similar (negative public attitude, insufficient aid of state and state institutions, the absence of a mediator, etc.) (Veniūtė, 2007).

It was already mentioned that the lack of education and the lack of professional preparation significantly hamper the entrenchment of people with disabilities in employment. Šėporaitytė D. and Tereškinas A. (2007) carried out the study in which disabled by different disabilities, representatives of various intermediary institutions, employers and experts of employment and educational problems were interviewed by semi-structured interview method; the study revealed that people with different disabilities have unequal access to education.

Lithuanian National Union of Students (LNUS) carried out the study in 2009 and this study revealed that improvement trend of people with disabilities in higher education continues, but the pace could be faster. The number of disabled students in Lithuania during this study year grew more slowly than in the past, Lithuania's high schools are still to be discovered by students with disabilities from other countries, and lack of funds is named as the main obstacle to improve conditions for disabled people (Lithuanian National Union of Students, 2009).

However, it should be noted that these studies further illustrate the situation of young people with disabilities in high schools, but do not disclose the opportunities of these population groups to join them. In this context it is believed that more attention should be paid to researches of young people with disabilities in comprehensive schools,

67

because the possibilities develop at this level; these possibilities determine their studies in high schools.

Youth

During the observation of the number of the young (up to 25 years old) unemployed over the past decades, it was noted that their record was achieved in 2000. More than 34 thousand youngsters were registered in exchange on the 1st of January in 2001. It has been said that the beginning of the 21st century was not favourable for the country's economy; the supply of labour was particularly impaired. Negative record was achieved repeatedly in 2010; the number of young unemployed exceeded 44 thousand at the end of the period.

In 2008, the after-effects of the economic downturn have not yet been strongly expressed, but youth unemployment increased the most. The youth unemployment rate was 25 percent in the first quarter of 2009; it increased by 44 percent during the quarter and it increased 2.5 times during the year (Changes of Unemployment Rate, 2009).

The relative proportion of young people was below 20 percent in the total population number since 1995. It is interesting to note that during the both periods of 2000 and 2010, i.e., when the total number of unemployed has reached its peak, the proportion of youth was slightly higher than ten percent. During the recovery of the labour market, the relative share of young people also varies quite marginally. This shows that despite the economic context, entrenchment in the labour market is a formidable obstacle for a certain number of young people.

Table 2.**The Number of Unemployed** (Lithuanian Labour Exchange data) (end of period, thousand)

	1994	1995	1996	1997	1998	1999	2000
Unemployed, of which:	78	127,7	109,4	120,2	122,8	177,4	225,9
youth (under 25 years old)	17,4	24	20,6	22,6	23,1	31,1	34,4
	2001	2002	2003	2004	2005	2006	2007
Unemployed, of which:	224	191,2	158,8	126,4	87,2	79,3	69,7
youth (under 25 years old)	28,7	21,7	17,2	10,3	5,8	6,4	6,4
	2008	2009	2010	2011	2012		
Unemployed, of which:	95,0	268,8	311,3	227,1	210,1		
youth (under 25 years old)	11,5	39,1	44,7	29,6	25,4*		

provisional data.

Most of the young unemployed who apply to the labour exchanges do not have professional preparation and work experience: according to Lithuanian Labour Exchange data, in 2012, unskilled young unemployed accounted for nearly 58 percent, while never worked – 56 percent (Portrait of the Young Unemployed, 2013).

A systematic analysis of problems (as entirety) of youth unemployment in Lithuania was accomplished in Okunevičiūtė-Neverauskienė (2006) thesis "Assessment of the socio-economic consequences of youth unemployment and its reduction". The analysis substantiates the existence of a close link between the general level of employment and youth age group employment rate. Her study showed that youth employment also declined during the period of 1997-2005 when overall employment of the population declined. However, as shown by the detailed statistical analysis of the data, changes in the labour market affected very differently different demographic groups – the decrease in employment mostly affected individuals from young people age group.

Table 3.**The Main Indicators of the Labour Market** (Statistics Lithuania data)

	2006	2007	2008	2009	2010	2011	2012
Activity level, (%)	55,9	56,3	56,7	57,7	56,8	57,4	57,7
Activity level, 15-24 years old (%)	*26,3*	*27,4*	*30,8*	*30,3*	*28,4*	*28,2*	*29,3*
Employment rate, (%)	5,6	4,3	5,8	13,7	17,8	15,4	13,4
Employment rate, 15-24 years old (%)	*9,8*	*8,2*	*13,4*	*29,2*	*35,7*	*32,6*	*26,7*
Unemployment rate, (%)	52,7	53,9	53,3	49,8	46,7	48,6	50
Unemployment rate, *15-24 years old (%)*	*23,7*	*25,2*	*26,7*	*21,5*	*18,3*	*19*	*21,5*
Long-term unemployed young people (6>months, thousand)	*5,9*	*3,8*	*5,4*	*19,4*	*24,9*	*22,4*	*15,4*
Proportion of 30-34 years old people with university education (%)	35,5	35,3	39,8	46,6	46,1	48,2	49,6

The economic loss due to the changes of youth situation in the labour market is evaluated in this dissertation; the economic loss is measured by GDP which is not created. A large potential benefit, which was not received, indicates that potential unemployment reduction opportunities were untapped in the economy. Although youth unemployment decrease should mean its major employment, but, instead of increasing the ranks of the employed, some of the young people added to the proportion of economically inactive population when they left the country's labour market during the investigation period. Also, the calculations showed that the increasing *emigration of young people* influenced the economic loss due to the employment decline. GDP, which is not created due to the country's population migration in 1997-2005, increased from 3.5 percent to 7.1 percent, including the age group of youth – from 4.0 percent to 9.1 percent. Thus, migration, in which younger people dominate, is an important factor which is slowing down Lithuania's economy growth. The results provide the opportunity to analyze and wider social consequences of unemployment: 68.6 percent respondents of the survey indicated that youth crime is a consequence of the conditions of life, and even 72.8 percent – that youth employment is a key factor in reducing crime (Pocius, Okunevičiūtė-Neverauskienė, 2005).

The study which was carried out in dissertation showed that youth unemployment is the result of insufficiently effective policy of education, vocational training (in the broad sense), social security, labour market and economy. It is motivated in the study, that during the solution of the problems of youth unemployment, the key is to ensure systematic and comprehensive solutions both developing the formation of youth work potential and its employment measures; a flexible integrated youth unemployment prevention and its mitigation system should start in comprehensive school and terminate in a variety of tax incentives for employers who recruit young people from the respective groups.

The above findings are confirmed or complemented by other studies in the country. A sociological survey of the situation of young people was carried out in 2005 (Spinter Research, 2005) and it revealed a complex situation of young people in the labour market. 36 percent young people who were interviewed worked during the investigation; the unemployed mostly told that they are learners. Most of those who were working claimed that they are satisfied with it; the majority worked full-time. The respondents worked both according to the specialty (36 percent) and not to the specialty (39 percent). 22 percent workers had no specialty. Most of the employees told that they are hired employees, 10 percent said that they have their own business.

During the examination of particularly vulnerable 15-29 years old youth groups in the labour market (convicts without prison sentences, persons undergoing treatment in addiction rehab centres, young people who eliminated from education system), a lot of attention has been paid for respondents' professional preparation and practical work experience, as these factors have a significant impact on situation of individuals in the labour market (Okunevičiūtė-Neverauskienė, Moskvina, 2008). The study showed that the majority of respondents did not have professional preparation, and even 44 percent of them did not have secondary education. Despite the low level of education, the vast

71

majority of respondents was able to boast of having although small but independent or wage-work experience.

The lack of professional preparation, dissatisfaction with the proposed wages and lack of work experience primarily determine their disadvantaged situation in the labour market. Higher education provides better opportunities of youth competition in the labour market (Okunevičiūtė-Neverauskienė, Moskvina, 2008; Okunevičiūtė-Neverauskienė et al., 2007b).

The analysis of the above target groups characteristics of unemployed youth and their problems of integration into the labour market was performed (Okunevičiūtė-Neverauskienė, Moskvina, 2008); this analysis has once again confirmed that professional preparation and work experience have a crucial role in achieving the employment. But without them, there are a lot of subjective factors which impede the beginning of employment or the return to it; these factors are lack of the general skills and social skills, dependencies, susceptibility to deviant behaviour, lack of awareness of opportunities in the labour market. It is believed that under favourable conditions in the labour market, removal of these barriers and prevention through both efforts of labour market institutions and social partners (especially the non-governmental sector) will effectively contribute to raising the economic activity of the young population of the country.

Young people often are a target group of studies which are aimed at workforce needs assessment. The requirements of employers for competencies of existing and potential employees are ascertained especially in detail. Personal characteristics of young people are of high importance for employers who recruit them without professional preparation (Šileika et al., 2005). The survey of employers opinion was carried out in 2007 (Rosinaitė et al., 2007) and it also revealed the importance of the general competencies during the integration into the labour market. According to the employers, general skills are one of the most important determinants of successful employment.

The studies presented above (Šileika et al., 2005; Rosinaitė et al., 2007; Okunevičiūtė-Neverauskienė et al., 2007b) indicate that the main barrier to youth participation in the labour market is the lack of professional preparation. The proportion of children and young people who are not participating in the education system is not decreasing. Prevention policy of early school leaving in Lithuania is directed to children under 16, because this age is associated to the limit for compulsory education. Some public interventions are provided to solve the problems of early exits from the education system, but these interventions are not consistently linked to the system. Reasons of early school leaving are complex and related to individual situation of the person. Therefore, on purpose to achieve effective prevention policy it is not sufficient to apply measures by improving provision of education services; it is necessary to combine those measures with measures from other policy areas – social, employment, crime prevention, etc. (Public Policy and Management Institute, 2007).

Older People

Despite the fact that statistics show that unemployment rate of 55-64 years old persons is usually lower than the national average, the target group of the elderly is experiencing difficulties in the labour market. The study "The Impact of Labour Market Policy Measures on Employment in Different Cycle Conditions of Economic Development" (2011-2013) confirms that during the growth of demand for labour 50 years old and older people return to the labour market more harder in comparison with other unemployed. It is necessary to remember that the proportion of the unskilled persons is quite significant among the older unemployed. In addition, it should be noted that the number of older unemployed women declined more slowly than the number of older unemployed men during favourable economic period. Older people have became "more marketable" in the labour market just at the beginning of labour deficit.

Figure 2. **Unemployed Persons by Age Groups** (Statistics Lithuania data, thousand)

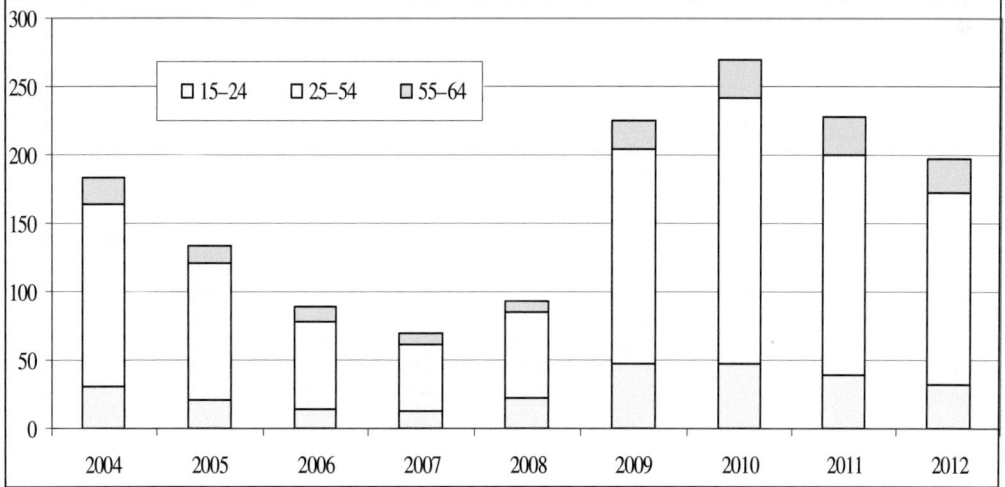

Statistics Lithuania carried out the study of the transition from work to retirement in 2012; 50-69 years old population was surveyed during this study (Ambrozaitiené, 2012). 4.7 thousand 50-69 years old population was interviewed during the study. Almost one-third (31.2 percent) 50-69 years old population who receives pension or is entitled to it said that they will continue to work or look for a work even when they are receiving the old-age pension; even 84.6 percent of them – for financial reasons. Almost a quarter (23.8 percent) 50-59 years old and more than half (56.1 percent) 60-69 years old population indicated that would cease employment immediately after receiving retirement or prior to receiving. Information about the wish of the employed and unemployed residents of this age to continue working was provided during the study. The study showed that every tenth (10.2 percent) 50-69 years old unemployed and recipient of an old-age pension man and every ninth (8.5 percent) unemployed and recipient of an old-age pension woman of this age would want to remain employed.

As can be seen, Statistics Lithuania survey data shows a fairly high level of older people's motivation to work, which could be enhanced by greater vocational training opportunities (allow to improve the qualification), a wider choice of atypical forms of employment and job application for altered older physical capabilities.

Something else could be said about the older people who are registered in the labour exchange. The survey "The Analysis of the Situation of Hardly Integrated People in the Labour Market and Tools to Enhance Their Employment" (Gruževskis et al., 2006b; Gruževskis et al., 2007) showed that usually older unemployed, who are registered in the labour exchange, are not a very large reserve that could supplement the labour market later in retirement age.

The study was based on the sociological survey of the elderly (55 years old and older) unemployed who were registered in the labour exchanges. It is observed that it is rather difficult for the elderly (55 years old and older) unemployed to engage in an active employment. During the analysis of the distribution of respondents by professional preparation it is seen that even 47 percent respondents who participated in the survey had not acquired any profession and 53 percent respondents had professional preparation. The changed conditions of production and new technologies depreciate education diploma and force to get a new vocation or qualification. It is therefore necessary to develop their lifelong learning opportunities, promote professional and territorial mobility, and help to gain new and marketable skills or specialty.

Older unemployed who are registered in the labour exchange are perhaps the worst materially made population layer in Lithuania. Their qualification is low. Therefore, employers often offer them extremely low wages. In addition, approximately every second older unemployed was registered in the labour exchange not for job search reasons. This is an alarming fact. Their motivation of vocational training / retraining is also poor. Gruževskis et al. (2006b) stated that the employment of older persons is limited by the workplaces which are not adapted to them, frequent breach of health and safety requirements, and too poor application of flexible forms of work organization. Therefore, the role of social partnership is emphasized during the provision of employment services for the elderly (55 years old and older).

It can be concluded that the motivation of the older customers of the labour exchanges is weak – a good part focuses as soon as possible to complete their working careers and does not plan to participate in the labour market in retirement age. During the development of people involvement in the labour market it would be important to create opportunities for retired continuously remain employed, because later this motivation falls (Gruževskis et al., 2006b). This conclusion is indirectly confirmed by the results of the study "The Needs of Older Population of Lithuania in Employment, Education, and Culture Areas" (Gruževskis et al., 2006a).

It should be noted that the majority of unemployed pensioners who were surveyed were satisfied with the fact that during the study did not work (61 percent), and only 14 percent said that they did not work and were not satisfied with that. According to the answers of the respondents, it can be assumed that only about 15 percent seniors are potentially ready to return to the labour market. Thus, the motivation of the older population to work is low enough. Training and education services are relevant for older people (2 thousand 60 years old and older people were interviewed during the study), but they have little interest in opportunities of the integration into the labour market (Gruževskis et al., 2006a).

Elderly people belong to the group whose members the worst employ after active labour market policy (ALMP) measures. The study of The Effectiveness of Active Labour Market Policy Measures (Okunevičiūtė-Neverauskienė et al., 2007a) shows that only the long-term unemployed are employed worse than 50 years old and older persons after the Lithuanian Labour Exchange ALMP measures (supported employment, assistance for job creation). It should be noted that a large part of ALMP participants have both these employment support features at the same time, which further complicates their process of the integration into the labour market. The study showed that older individuals also most of all devalue their chances in the labour market (Okunevičiūtė-Neverauskienė et al., 2007a).

Conclusion

The studies demonstrated that the problems of persons of risk groups have a complex character in the labour market. However, it can be noted that a large-scale study should be based on this provision; this kind of study is appropriate to include on purpose to identify processes how the economic situation, social and cultural environment, traditions of social security, education and vocational training, the degree of tolerance in the society, territorial economic features, the degree of sociality, perception of social solidarity in society and other factors affect behaviour, mindset, opportunities and their perception of individuals who are attributed to risk groups in the labour market.

Studies have revealed a lack of institutional co-operation, thus, a wide opportunity of analysis opens for management and public policy scientists. There is a reason to believe that factors which have the above individual nature much more influence the situation of persons of risk groups in the labour market than it is currently assumed.

The results of measures for evaluations of various social projects are an important source of qualitative information, but in order to objectively assess the situation at the country level, it is essential to create a reliable and operational monitoring system of persons of risk groups. For example, it is important to take advantage of statistics during the analysis of fluctuation trends of the situation of people with disabilities in the labour market. However, there is a lack of relevant information about the situation of this risk group. It should be noted that the information is rapidly changing in social and economic environment, thus, there is a lack of operational information which characterizes the situation of persons of all risk groups in the labour market to a country's extent. Probably the only more readily available source of information is the Lithuanian Labour Exchange (LLE) data, but it does not reflect the real situation in the country, because only a small part of persons from risk groups registers in it. On the other hand, LLE fairly narrowly captures different social risk factors. It is particularly problematic to get information about the situation of persons of different nationalities in the labour market, these data are not collected.

List of References

1. Ambrozaitienė D. „Perėjimas nuo darbinės veiklos prie pensijos". Lietuvos statistikos departamentas (2012). Prieiga per internetą: http://web.stat.gov.lt/lt/news/view/?id=10421&PHPSESSID=14b1ef643468e1d8e7d28161dda3d14a

2. Bikmanienė R.; Andriušaitienė D.; Šileika A.; Gruževskis B. *Asmenų su klausos negalia įsidarbinimo galimybių tyrimas*. Tyrimo ataskaita. Darbo ir socialinių tyrimų institutas. (2007a).

3. Gruževskis B., Okunevičiūtė Neverauskienė L., Česnuitytė V. „Asmenų, neturinčių pagrindinio išsilavinimo, integracijos į Lietuvos darbo rinką problemos". *Socialinis darbas*, Nr. 6 (2). Vilnius: Mykolo Romerio universitetas, p. 87-94. ISNN 1648-4789. (2007).

4. Gruževskis B.; Okunevičiūtė-Neverauskienė L.; Biveinytė S. *Vyresnio amžiaus Lietuvos gyventojų poreikiai užimtumo, švietimo ir kultūros srityse*. II ir III mokslinio tyrimo etapų ataskaitos. Darbo ir socialinių tyrimų institutas. (2006a).

5. Gruževskis B.; Okunevičiūtė-Neverauskienė L.; Žalimienė L.; Česnuitytė V. *Sunkiai integruojamų asmenų padėties darbo rinkoje analizė ir priemonės jų užimtumui didinti*. Mokslinio tyrimo ataskaita. Darbo ir socialinių tyrimų institutas. (2006b). Prieiga per internetą: http://www.ldb.lt/Informacija/Apie/Documents/sunkiai_integruojami.pdf.

6. *Jauno bedarbio portretas*. Jaunimo situacija darbo rinkoje. Lietuvos darbo birža (Lithuanian labour exchange) 2013. Prieiga per internetą: http://www.ldb.lt/jaunimui/naudinga/Puslapiai/bed_portretas.aspx

7. Lietuvos darbo birža. www.ldb.lt

8. Lietuvos studentų sąjunga. *Studentai su negalia Lietuvos aukštosiose mokyklose 2009m.* (2009). Prieiga per internetą: http://www.ndt.lt/news/id-tyrimas_studentai_su_negalia_lietuvos_aukstosiose_mokyklose_2009.html

9. Matiušaitytė R. *Darbo rinkos probleminės grupės ir jų padėties gerinimas*. Daktaro disertacija. (2001).

10. *Moterys ir vyrai Lietuvos visuomenėje – 2009: Moterų ir vyrų padėties pokyčių visose srityse išplėstinis tyrimas ir vertinimas*. Tyrimo ataskaita. Moterų informacijos centras. Vilnius. (2009).

11. Nedarbo lygio pokyčiai. Pranešimas spaudai. Lietuvos statistikos departamentas. (2009) Prieiga per internetą: http://web.stat.gov.lt/lt/news/view/?id=7742&PHPSESSID=twmjcujxideyz

12. Neįgaliųjų socialinės integracijos įstatymas. Nr. IX-2228, 2004-05-11, Žin., 2004, Nr. 83-2983 (2004-05-22). (2004).

13. Okunevičiūtė Neverauskienė L.; Gruževskis B.; Moskvina J.; Pocius A.; Šileika A.; Šlekienė K. *Aktyvios darbo rinkos politikos priemonių efektyvumo tyrimas.* Darbo ir socialinių tyrimų institutas. (2007a). Prieiga per internetą: http://www.ldb.lt/Informacija/Apie/Documents/ADRPP%20efektyvumo%20tyrim as.pdf

14. Okunevičiūtė-Neverauskienė L.. *Jaunimo nedarbo socialinių ekonominių pasekmių vertinimas bei jo mažinimas.* Daktaro disertacijos santrauka. (2006).

15. Okunevičiūtė-Neverauskienė L.; Gruževskis B.; Pocius A.; Moskvina J. *Jaunimo įsitvirtinimo Lietuvos darbo rinkoje galimybių tobulinimas.* Studija. Darbo ir socialinių tyrimų institutas (2007b).

16. Okunevičiūtė-Neverauskienė L.; Moskvina J. „Socialiai pažeidžiamo jaunimo problemos integracijos į darbo rinką kontekste". *Filosofija. Sociologija,* T. 19, Nr. 2, p. 41–54. (2008).

17. Okunevičiūtė-Neverauskienė L.; Moskvina J. *Darbo rinkos politikos priemonių poveikis užimtumui įvairiomis ekonomikos raidos ciklo sąlygomis.* Mokslinio tyrimo ataskaita. Lietuvos socialinių tyrimų centro Darbo ir socialinių tyrimų institutas. Vilnius. (2011-2013)

18. Okunevičiūtė-Neverauskienė L.; Pocius A.; Gruževskis B.; Moskvina J.; Junevicius R. *Neįgaliesiems taikomų aktyvių darbo rinkos politikos priemonių vertinimas ir pasiūlymų parengimas projekte įgyvendinamų priemonių efektyvumui didinti.* Tyrimo santrauka. Darbo ir socialinių tyrimų institutas. (2008). Prieiga per internetą: http://www.ldb.lt/Informacija/Apie/Documents/mtyrimas_neigaliuju_ADRPP_200 80723.pdf

19. Pocius A., Okunevičiūtė Neverauskienė L. „Ekonominio nuostolio dėl Lietuvos darbo rinkos pokyčių įvertinimas". *Pinigų studijos,* Nr.2. Vilnius: Lietuvos bankas, 2005, ISNN 1392-2637, p. 30 – 46. (2005).

20. Rosinaitė V.; Bernotas D.; Biveinytė S.; Blažienė I.; Česnuitytė V., Gražulis V., Gruževskis B.; Misiūnas A.; Pocius A.; Stancikas E.; Šileika A.; Šlekienė K.; Zabarauskaitė R. *Magistrantų integracijos į darbo rinką monitoringo sistemos sukūrimas.* Studija. (2007).

21. Skučienė D.; Šumskaitė L. *Neįgaliųjų darbo rinkos analizė.* Tyrimo ataskaita. (2005). Prieiga per internetą: http://www.equal.lt/uploads/docs/VB-13%20Darbo_rinkos_analize_-_tyrimo_ataskaita.pdf

22. Spinter tyrimai. *Jaunimo situacijos sociologinis tyrimas.* Tyrimo ataskaita. (2005).

23. Statistics Lithuania. Database. Užimtieji ir samdomieji (Employed and employees by economic activity). Available at: http://db1.stat.gov.lt/statbank/default.asp?w=1360

24. Šėporaitytė D., Tereškinas A. *Neįgaliųjų įsidarbinimo ir mokslo galimybės Lietuvoje*. Tyrimo ataskaita. (2007).

25. Šileika A.; Gruževskis B.; Kabaila A.; Pocius A.; Zabarauskaitė R.; Česnuitytė V.; Junevičius R. 2005. *Sisteminis koncerno „Achemos grupė", kaip gamybinio vieneto, darbo jėgos atitikimo rinkos poreikiams tyrimas*. Tyrimo ataskaita. (2005).

26. Veniūtė M. Psichikos negalią turinčių žmonių socialinės integracijos galimybės Lietuvoje" Daktaro disertacija. *Biologinė psichiatrija ir psichofarmakologija,*2007, T. 9, Nr. 2, p. 88. (2007). Prieiga per internetą: http://www.pri.kmu.lt/Biologine%20psichiatrija(zurnalas)/zurnalas2007_2.htm

27. Viešosios politikos ir vadybos institutas. *Ankstyvojo pasitraukimo iš švietimo sistemos prevencija*. Tyrimo ataskaita. (2007). Prieiga per internetą: http://www.smm.lt/svietimo_bukle/docs/tyrimai/es/ankstyvojo%20pasitraukimo%20prevencija_ataskaita.pdf

28. Žalimienė L.; Lazutka R.; Skučienė D.; Bagdonas A.; Šumskaitė L. *2005 metais įvykusio invalidumo nustatymo ir su tuo susijusių išmokų skyrimo reformos analizė*. Mokslinio tyrimo ataskaita. (2007).

Trend in the development of employment and unemployment according to gender and age of the population in Lithuania and the evaluation of integration into the labour market

A. Pocius

Labour and Social Research Institute

B. Gruževskis

Vilnius University

This article assesses trends in the development of employment and unemployment according to gender and age of the population in Lithuania; the priority is given to monitor changes in different population groups in the labour market during the different economic development cycle conditions. Employing comparative analysis method, the publication valued the opportunities of women, men, the elderly, and young people to integrate into the labour market; the opportunities were linked with the promotion of the activity of these groups. The exclusion of the labour market target groups is an important problem; these groups are essential objects of the comparative study in this publication. The publication also analyzes the role of active labour market measures during the process of integration of the country's unemployed into the labour market; the factors of employment are considered highlighting the potential impact of innovations to improve the situation in the labour market.

Keywords: integration, employment, unemployment, labour market, economic development, labour market policy, long term unemployment.

Introduction

Descending the number of young people to likely engage into the labour market in Lithuania, as in other European countries, the elderly forms an increasing segment of the population every year. The relative weight of young people which could potentially be involved into the labour market will reduce because of the ageing of the workers in the country. At the same time, the ageing trends of population monitored in Lithuania should at least formally establish optimum conditions under which the youth would be employed. In prospect, the young people in the labour market can become a "deficit". However, the observed trend is that the ageing of the population at present does not automatically guarantee a successful integration of young people into the labour market, because educational institutions still qualify many specialists with not very marketable professions; young people do not have enough skills and they lack experience. In this situation, the elderly who have marketable professions get stronger role in the labour market. It is important that the country's obsolescent labour market would adapt to current challenges. This results in the importance of trends of analyses of employment and unemployment according to the key demographic groups. The questions of the integration of women into the labour market are quite sensitive. Labour market policy seeks to reduce the differences of the labour market indicators for gender and to promote greater use of flexible forms of employment for women which seek to be employed.

This article aims to examine the factors influencing employment, to discuss the role of active labour market measures in the process of the country's unemployed into the labour market, to evaluate opportunities of the integration of different groups into the labour market, the trends of employment and activity and changes in unemployment, to examine the differences of regional indices changes between urban and rural.

Factors Influencing Employment

According to classical labour market theory, the balance between labour supply and demand determines the employment[23]. However, different authors note that perfect competition cannot be in the theory level of labour market because of the specifics of the labour resources as an exchange object and dual nature of the labour resources: working as an economic category (determinable law of marginal utility), and working as a social category (determinable laws and cultural and moral norms). It should also be noted that when influencing the employment of the population, the relationship between economic and social factors changes depending on the historical period, the political situation in the

---

[23]Barro R.J. *Macroeconomics*. Fourth Edition. John Wiley and Sons, Inc. New York(1993, p.145-162).

country, as well as fluctuations in economic cycles (economic growth or recession). Without going into analysis of a lengthy historical changes in Lithuanian labour market, it should be noted that employment situation has changed significantly in all spheres in Lithuania after the restoration of independence: the total number of employees and the level of employment has reduced, especially the employment of women and people of retirement age has reduced, employment in industry has reduced and employment in services has increased, employment in the public sector has reduced and employment in the private sector and number of employers has increased, etc. Gradually, a market economy relationship has started to develop in the country, although it should be noted that Soviet-era law heavily influenced labour employment for a long time. And even in 2013, according to the World Competitiveness Index, employment and dismissal practice of Lithuania are on 130 place (out of 148 countries) and redundancy costs are on 111 place[24]. However, comparing the position in Lithuanian labour market in 2007 and 2010, it can be concluded that the regulation of labour relations has enough limited impact on overall employment. In 2007, significantly higher overall employment rate was achieved via less flexible labour relations than after the liberalization of labour relations in 2009-2010 (male employment rate of 59.8 and women 48.9 percent, and, respectively, 49.8 and 46 percent in 2010). However, it was already mentioned that employment is a complex category, so its change cannot be measured by change of one or more factors. Factors which influence labour supply and labour demand should be distinguished when the factors which determine employment are overall assessed.

Factors Determining Labour Supply

Such core group of factors determines labour supply:

- demographic factors;
- the level of wages;
- social benefits;
- education and qualifications;
- working conditions (job attractiveness);

---

[24]*The Global Competitiveness Report 2013-2014.* Word Economic Forum (2013). Available at:http://reports.weforum.org/the-global-competitiveness-report-2013-2014/.

- motivation for work (occupational expectations);
- mobility.

Each of the above factors will be briefly discussed.

Demographic factors. Since 2000, demographic processes make an increasingly negative impact on Lithuanian labour market and employment prospects. The total number of population, especially the working-age population, is decreasing because of the negative natural increase and especially intensive emigration; it reduces the supply of labour. Population ageing process is very fast in Lithuania due to the low birth rate and emigration of younger people; older people (50 +) constitute an increasing share of labour resources. This process is particularly rapid since 2011 when the demographic decline began in Lithuania and the increasingly smaller group of young people complements the working-age population. This trend will dominate the coming 11-12 years.

Level of wages and social benefits. Wages in our country grew up to the year 2008 when the economic downturn happened; Lithuania was in 20 place in the EU according to the average earnings before tax. In 2010, Lithuania dipped into the 23 place after the crisis, but wage growth was even lower in Lithuania than in Bulgaria and Romania, which were in 26 and 27 places. In 2012, average earnings in Lithuania amounted to 2173.68 LTL (gross), and "take-home pay" (net) – 1687.88 LTL. In 2012, the average old age pension was 815.57 LTL, the average unemployment social insurance benefit was 563.17 LTL, and basic social benefit was 130 LTL[25]. Given the fact that in 2012 real minimum standard of living was around 847 LTL, it can be said that both the social benefits and the level of wages in Lithuania is quite low. Bearing in mind that the EU15 average salary is about four times higher, one of the major causes of active emigration can be easily explained. In Lithuania MMW was 800 LTL (approximately 674 LTL "take-home pay") up to the year 2012, and very often there was no incentive for the recipients of social benefits to take a lower paid job, because the remuneration almost did not increase their total revenue (in addition to compensation for heating and benefits for children). MMW started to increase since 2012 and it amounted to 1000 LTL (gross) in 2013.

---

[25]Information is prepared by Ministry of Social Security and Labour of the Republic of Lithuania (2013).

Education and qualifications. Since the beginning of the twentieth century, the role of education for employment is increasing constantly in the macro and micro (individual) level. Economic globalization, in particular the use of information technologies in production, further accelerated this process. Rapid technological change has consistently promoted the actualization of knowledge and skills, and lifelong learning is becoming the norm. Matching education and skill is characterised by employment and labour supply issues:

- territorial level;
- time level;
- professional level.

In Lithuania there are problems in all three levels while training the residents in the sphere of career education. Educated professionals and workers are more and more concentrated in the major cities, and there is a growing shortage of skilled labour in other regions. On the other hand, with unemployment in Lithuania growing some skilled workers are leaving the country, and with the recovery process of the economy starting the shortage of the skilled labour supply is felt even more (about 40 percent employers declared that there was adequate skilled labour shortage in 2012[26]). Also, distorted professional and graduate-level system has a negative impact on employment in Lithuania. Academic studies and social science degree programs dominate, when a lack of skilled workers or technology and science professionals is felt the most.

Working conditions and work motivation. Working conditions are characterized by the nature of work (stress at work, work intensity), labour relations, working hours, wages and salaries. Low- and medium-tech jobs dominate in Lithuania, but at the economic policy level it is declared to encourage investment and to develop high-tech businesses and jobs. Labour relations in Lithuania can be described as tense. On the one hand, the social dialogue is developed very weakly in the country and distrust between employer and employee dominates in the companies. On the other hand, one of the most liberal wage-setting systems is in Lithuania (according to this indicator Lithuania occupies 7th place out

---

[26]Round Table Discussion in the European Commission Representation in Lithuania, Vilnius, 2013 09 04.

of 148 countries in the world)[27], and this directly affects the employment relationship. It was briefly mentioned the level of wages in Lithuania and it does not completely deter citizens from emigration when there are conditions of the free movement of labour. In conclusion, it may be noted that working conditions in Lithuania are not very attractive in the total EU backdrop and it negatively influences Lithuanian investment attractiveness and work motivation of the country's population. The "poverty trap", low pay transparency and wage discrepancy real effort at work (especially in the public sector) influence work motivation negatively. "Green" jobs are not sufficiently developed in Lithuania, the number of social and health care workers declines since 2011. In order to increase the motivation to work, in 2010-2012, opportunities to combine work and family commitments were improved, cash social assistance system was revised, and pre-school network was developed.

Mobility. It was already mentioned indirectly that very high mobility of the population, especially outer, occurs in Lithuania. Since 1990 till 2012, 711 thousand people went from Lithuania. Just after the crisis in 2010-2012, 158 thousand people left the country and 41 thousand people arrived. Labour supply and especially the supply of the qualified younger work force decline steadily in Lithuania; it is the result of external population mobility.

Factors Affecting Labour Demand

Demand for labour depends on:

- labour costs;
- labour productivity;
- demand for goods and services;
- production cycles;
- the number of jobs;
- employers' expectations.

---

[27]*The Global Competitiveness Report 2013-2014*. Word Economic Forum, 2013 Available at: http://reports.weforum.org/the-global-competitiveness-report-2013-2014/.

Labour costs. In EU context, the overall cost of labour in Lithuania is not high, while in respect of net earnings, social security contributions and other taxes are high enough that local employers are often unable to avoid the temptation to participate in the informal economy (it often corresponds to economic interest of employees who receive the social benefits).

Labour productivity. Labour productivity in Lithuania lags behind the EU average. However, we are of the opinion that the indicator calculation methodology which is applied does not meet the real conditions, as analysis of multinationals performance shows that it is paid less for the same work in Lithuania. On the other hand, if average wage amounted to 25-28 percent EU average in 2011, then GDP per capita in purchasing power parity was 62 percent. Accordingly, the labour productivity in Lithuania is about 60 percent EU-27 average, but Lithuania's population receives almost two times less money for the same job.

Employers' expectations. This factor has a great influence on the formation of labour demand in Lithuania; as it was already mentioned, the salary is little regulated and largely depends on the employer's control. On the other hand, employers' expectations have much influence on employing employees according to their career readiness. Employers in Lithuania are reluctant to employ graduates; instead of graduates they are searching staff with practical skills. On the other hand, high requirements are often raised for new employees and the employers expect competencies (management, accounting skills, foreign language skills, sales expertise, and so on) from new employees. However, the surveys[28] of Lithuania employers showed that usually short-term 1-3 years personnel policy, which is highly dependent on market fluctuations, is carried out in companies. Employers are wary of investing in the training of the staff and are little developing means of corporate social responsibility.

Influence of other factors depends primarily on production cycles. Employment protection mechanisms operate weakly in economic downturn conditions in Lithuania, so unemployment in all age groups and occupations rapidly increases. Employment starts to grow after 1-2 years with the condition of the growing economy, but long-term unemployment increases, the greater part of employers cannot meet their labour needs quickly and on the appropriate scope. Regardless of the level of unemployment, 10-15

---

[28]Labour and Social Research Institute conducted a variety of research surveys in 2002-2012.

thousand openings are constantly in Lithuania; low feeing (1000-1300 LTL) and the territorial discrepancies usually determine their non-filling[29].

The Influence of Innovations on Employment Growth

Currently, innovations are the major and most effective means to increase employment in Lithuania and other EU countries. Innovations can have a positive impact on the labour force supply and demand. Appropriate innovations policy can ensure the effective use of local labour resources and their attraction from abroad or from other areas, increase work motivation of the population and satisfaction at work (positively influencing wages and working conditions), and reduce differences between the territorial employment opportunities and unemployment (Table 1).

It is important to note that in order to ensure effective use of innovations in employment, it is necessary to combine the most appropriate financial and organizational arrangements with the training programs. Shortage of a properly designed and skilled labour in Lithuania restricts business development increasingly.

It should also be noted that a variety of purposeful innovations can effectively contribute to one or the other population employment. Use of information technologies and the development of services are constantly increasing employment of women and older workers and their work motivation. In order to increase the employment of this population, it is purposeful to reduce the physical work demands in industrial processes and to increase teleworking and flexible work options through the medium of innovations. This will not only enhance the attractiveness of employment, but also reduce costs of non-productive time and workplace organization.

---

[29]Data of Lithuanian Labour Exchange.

Table 1.**The Influence of Innovations on Increasing Labour Supply**

Factors Determining Labour Supply	Impact of Innovations	The Change of Factor Determining Labour Supply
Wage level	Increases productivity, increases service or product diversity, increases the value of the work	Results in terms of wage growth
Education and qualifications	Introduces new technologies, brings new businesses	Demand for skilled labour increases, offers the possibility of in-service training
Working conditions	Unattractive jobs decline	Working conditions improve and the attractiveness of jobs increases
Work motivation	The above-listed changes	Increases the attractiveness of employment and satisfaction with the work
Labour mobility	The above-listed changes	Can reduce or increase the demand for labour and its territorial formation depending on the specific measures

Source: developed by the authors.

Innovations affect the demand for labour. Processes and work organization mostly are improved by the support of innovations in order to increase productivity, reduce labour costs and to market new products or services. It can be maintained that the dominant purpose of innovations is to increase profits, so as a result the employment cannot only to not increase, but to decrease. This issue must be analyzed and programmed separately, and, if necessary, combining innovations employment issues with other market participants, and especially employment services (Lithuanian Labour Exchange), local authorities and NGOs in order to increase the impact of innovations on employment growth. However, cooperation with the local employment service agencies can ensure most benefits for organizers of innovations. The work force compliance costs for jobs which are created can be reduced and the social effectiveness of innovations can be increased by combining innovations with active labour market policies which are implemented by the employment services.

The Role of Active Labour Market Measures in the Process of the Country's Unemployed into the Labour Market

It was already mentioned the use of the active labour market policy measures when suitable labour resources were supplied for innovations and these innovations were combined. However, options of active labour market policy measures (ALMPM) are much broader. They improve labour supply and increase its relevance to real labour market conditions, promote the demand for labour (especially from the population which is more difficult to employ) and reduce structural unemployment. *Vocational training, retraining and in-service training programs* play a significant role in ALMPM structure. They are long-term in nature in regard to increasing employment, but they impact the employment indirectly. In order to maximize their effectiveness and impact on employment in most cases:

- Vocational training programs are offered just for those persons who have no profession, mostly young people;
- Training and employment contracts are made; unemployed who have employers' agreement for employment after completing the program are sent to training programs.

Such a strict regulation of vocational training of unemployed is often criticized under market economy conditions, but these programs are one of the most expensive in ALMPM system, so tighter regulation and control enables greater savings[30].

---

[30]Gruževskis B., Kabaila A., Bagdžiūnienė D., Okunevičiūtė Neverauskienė L. *Bedarbių profesinio mokymo naudos tyrimas, įvertinant mokymo programų vykdymo efektyvumą bei praktinio mokymo kokybę*. Report of the research. Labour and Social Research Institute, Vilnius (2006).

Another group of measures is *the employment support or subsidies to employers*. The employer may obtain all or part of the employee-pay and the financial resources to pay the applicable fees when hiring the unemployed. This measure is also often criticized and it is maintained that employers recruit workers who are supported, but dismiss others, which are not subsidized[31]. However, studies of Labour and Social Research Institute suggest[32] that individual groups of the unemployed (especially long-term unemployed and people with disabilities) have little chance to employ without such kind of support. Also, means of employment support help to engage older age (55 +) unemployed and women who return to the labour market after parental leave.

Public works programs can also be attributed to the employment support, but they have their own specifics, so they are often shown in a separate ALMPM group. Public works programs usually are of shorter-term and their goal is not long-term employment, but rather the support for work motivation and socially useful activities. Clearly, there are no restrictions that public works would be organized as a long-term national program, but municipalities and private employers (usually larger companies) organize them most commonly in Lithuania, so public works are more local, short-term in nature. On the other hand, public works programs are available to all groups of the unemployed, they can be modified by the unemployed capabilities (eg. the disabled), or they can be combined with participation in other ALMPM (eg. vocational training).

Workplace creation measures. This is also one of the most expensive ALMPM. These measures are applied vey narrowly in Lithuania, allowing only for people with disabilities to find a job. The researches, which were carried out in Austria, Ireland and the Netherlands, have shown that job creation measures can also be effective, and can adequately secure employment of separate groups, if these measures are not developed in a massive way and if they are more adapted to the opportunities of specific unemployed and local labour market needs.

---

[31]Okunevičiūtė Neverauskienė L., Moskvina J. *Aktyvios darbo rinkos politikos priemonių socialinė nauda.* Philosophy. Sociology. Vilnius (2010, p. 101-111).
[32]Gruževskis B., Kabaila A., Moskvina J., Okunevičiūtė Neverauskienė L.*Bedarbių užimtumo rėmimas. Užimtumo rėmimo programų efektyvumo vertinimas.*Vilnius, Labour and Social Research Institute(2006).

Self-employment promotion measures. This group of measures gets least negative evaluations from all groups of measures. On the one hand, their implementation does not require greater financial resources, on the other – it provides better and longer-term employment effects because there is low number of the most vulnerable groups of unemployed[33] among the participants in these measures. Utility of self-employment measures shows itself in the fact that they are most able to adapt to local labour market needs and opportunities of unemployed, i.e. local labour market helps to ensure the highest accuracy of using these measures.

In conclusion, it may be noted that ALMPM regardless of their varying effects have a positive impact on the integration of the unemployed into the labour market and increase the opportunities in employment of different population groups. The researches, which were carried out in Lithuania and other EU countries, have shown that the efficiency of ALMPM depends on education, age and the place of residence of the unemployed. The younger and more educated unemployed use options of ALMPM more successfully, as well as urban population. Older people, especially in rural areas, have fewer opportunities to participate in ALMPM.

Participation in ALMPM has been actively developed in Lithuania until 2008, and, for example, participation in ALMPM was offered for about 80 percent registered unemployed in 2005 (Table 2). When the crisis started, this number dropped to 12.8 percent in 2009. The number of people who were sent to ALMPM increased slightly, whereas the total number of unemployed was rising. There were about 60 thousand unemployed in 2010-2011, and 64.7 thousand in 2012, it accounted for only about 20 percent of the total number of registered unemployed.

---

[33]Moskvina J., Okunevičiūtė Neverauskienė L.*Aktyvi darbo rinkos politika: teorija ir praktika.* Vilnius, Vilnius Gediminas Technical University (2011, p. 52).

Table 2. **Total Number and the Percentage of Registered, Employed and Directed to ALMPM in 2005-2012**

Rate	2005	2006	2007	2008	2009	2010	2011	2012
Registered unemployed	163.9	160.8	166.7	214.2	369.4	303.1	256.7	330.8
Employed	109.7	99.7	111.9	122.6	121.8	191.2	218.8	202.6
Employed, %	*66.93*	*62.00*	*67.13*	*57.24*	*32.97*	*63.08*	*85.24*	*61.25*
Sent to ALMPM	129.9	99.8	72.1	36.3	47.5	59.3	59.7	64.7
Sent to ALMPM, %	*79.26*	*62.06*	*43.25*	*16.95*	*12.86*	*19.56*	*23.26*	*19.56*

Source: Data from Lithuanian Labour Exchange.

It should also be noted that Lithuanian ALMPM structure has changed after the economic crisis (Figure 1), participation of the unemployed in vocational training measures has decreased, whereas participation in public works has increased. At the same time, proportion between women and men who participate in different measures has changed.

Women were much more active in the ALMPM (Table 3) before the crisis, for example, they accounted for nearly 57 percent among all people who were sent to ALMPM in 2008, and only 45 percent[34] in 2012. In particular, women participation in vocational training programs (from 54 percent in 2008 up to 36 percent in 2012, and their absolute number decreased from 5000 to 900), and subsidized employment (from 65 percent up to 50 percent) decreased during the period of 2008-2012.

---

[34]Data from Lithuanian Labour Exchange.

Figure 1. **Participation of the Unemployed in ALMPM Measures in 2005-2012**
(in percent and thousands)

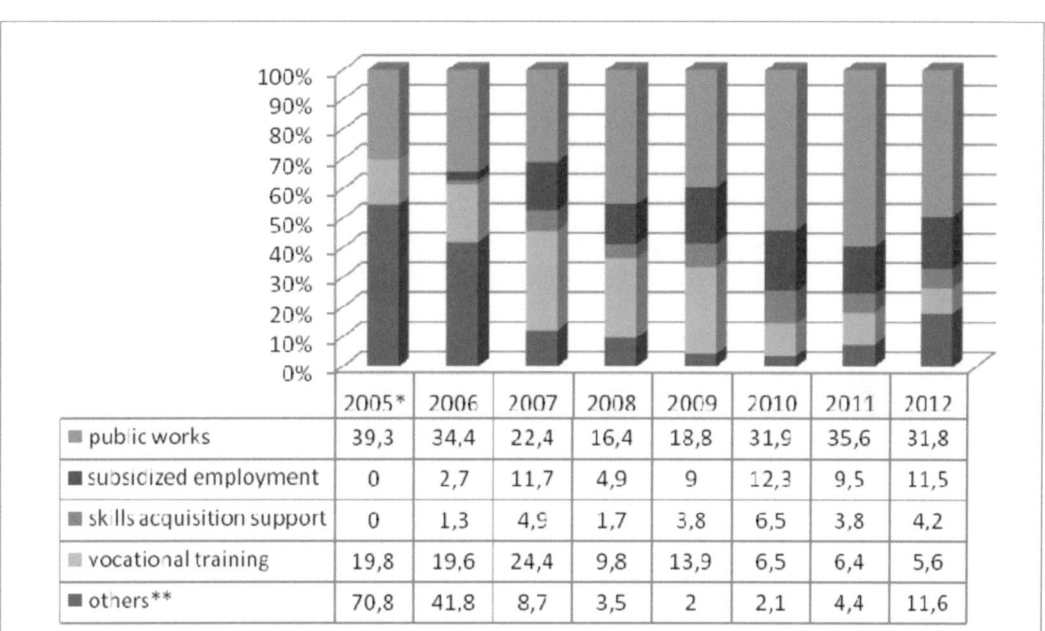

	2005*	2006	2007	2008	2009	2010	2011	2012
■ public works	39,3	34,4	22,4	16,4	18,8	31,9	35,6	31,8
■ subsidized employment	0	2,7	11,7	4,9	9	12,3	9,5	11,5
■ skills acquisition support	0	1,3	4,9	1,7	3,8	6,5	3,8	4,2
■ vocational training	19,8	19,6	24,4	9,8	13,9	6,5	6,4	5,6
■ others**	70,8	41,8	8,7	3,5	2	2,1	4,4	11,6

skills acquisition support, subsidized employment, and some other measures have not yet been introduced in 2005.

**support for workplace creation, measures of job rotation, vocational rehabilitation, and territorial mobility.*

Source: data from Lithuanian Labour Exchange.

The elderly (50 +) unemployed participation in ALMPM also decreased. 50 + unemployed amounted 32 percent among the participants in ALMPM in 2008, and only 26 percent in 2012. The number of older unemployed decreased in all groups of measures, but the biggest decrease was in vocational training (from 13 percent in 2008 to 7 percent (165 people) in 2012) and in subsidized employment (from 49 percent to 26 percent). Public works programs are the most accessible ones to the older unemployed; the part of the unemployed fell from 49 percent to 31 percent in these programs.

In the future, in order to increase employment, innovation can be directed into ALMPM improvement and, for this purpose, it is appropriate to use financial resources from EU structural assistance for 2014-2020. In Lithuania, according to the common EU priorities, at first, it should be invested in the improvement of diversity, quality and accessibility of Lithuanian Labour Exchange services. Innovation (more managerial and administrative) which increase equivalence of applicable measures for opportunities of the unemployed, i.e. which ensure greater differentiation of application and social sensitivity, would be very useful in this area. We are of the opinion that there should be created such possibilities that it would be possible to at most correspond and respond to work motivation of unemployed. It is true to say that the whole system of ALMPM should shape and maintain the work motivation of unemployed.

Table 3. Participation of the Unemployed in Active Labour Market Policy Measures in 2008 and 2012 (in thousands of people)

Year 2012					
	Total	Vocational training	Employment subsidies	Public works	Job rotation
Total	58.8	2.5	11.5	29.8	0.389
Women	26.7	0.9	5.8	13.4	0.344
Youth	11.8	0.8	3.8	3.3	0.087
50 +	15	0.165	2.2	10.3	0.026
Year 2008					
	Total	Vocational training	Employment subsidies	Public works	Job rotation
Total	31.1	9.2	4.9	11.9	0.385
Women	17.6	5.0	3.2	6.5	0.358
Youth	4.9	2.7	0.4	0.6	0.083
50 +	9.9	1.2	2.4	5.5	0.039

Source: data from Lithuanian Labour Exchange.

Observed tension shows that the integration of the unemployed into the labour market remains a major socio-economic problem. Labour and Social Research Institute have carried out the study on the effect of labour market policy measures in 2011-2013. The results of the study suggest that the application of active labour market measures in different economic cycle conditions played an important role in the process of integration of the unemployed, despite the previously expressed thoughts about the lack of unemployed people's activity (motivation to work). Regression analysis showed that the activity of the unemployed in the labour market during their participation in ALMPM in the last decade has let to achieve a positive result of the unemployment reduction. ALMPMs efficiency asserts itself in statistically significant effect in reducing importance of the level of unemployment.

The bigger number of workplaces which were occupied has also significantly decreased the unemployment rate. It is obvious that the unemployment rate is lower when more people are employed, but a favourable economic environment allows not only better financial conditions for greater number of people to include into the ALMPM, but also significantly improved relative opportunities for persons who participate in the ALMPM to employ by filling openings. In this way, the economic component of the unemployment rate is stronger than the component of the active policy (active measures).

The activity of the unemployed in the labour market, when they participated in measures, was chosen as a result variable in a regression analysis; an important conclusion was formulated. Growth of the number of social benefits receivers significantly reduces the activity of the unemployed in the labour market. This is evidenced by a strong inverse (negative) relationship between relative indices of the activity of the unemployed in the labour market and the dynamics of social benefits receivers. In other words, the number of recipients of social benefits grows because the unemployed seek to live more on social benefits but not to register into the labour exchange to participate in active measures. The social support system, which existed in Lithuania, was far from discouraging job-seekers to actively engage into the labour market. In this way, a kind of "de-motivating trap" forms because there are few levers which would push persons which seek to live on welfare to integrate into the labour market.

It is reasonable to assume that countries with a higher unemployment should spend more money on active labour market policies. However, the authors' calculations show that, in fact, it depended on the actual policy priorities and financial capabilities when economic crisis occurred in EU countries. The number of unemployed has increased and during the economic downturn Lithuania got the worst group of 6, where the unemployment rate was more than 13 percent. Nevertheless, in 2009, very few funding for active measures in this group of countries has been designed – only 0.3 percent GDP (Fig. 2).

Figure 2. **Grouping of the EU and other European Countries by the Rate of Unemployment in Terms of Expenditure on GDP in the Labour Market Policy Measures in 2009** (in percent)

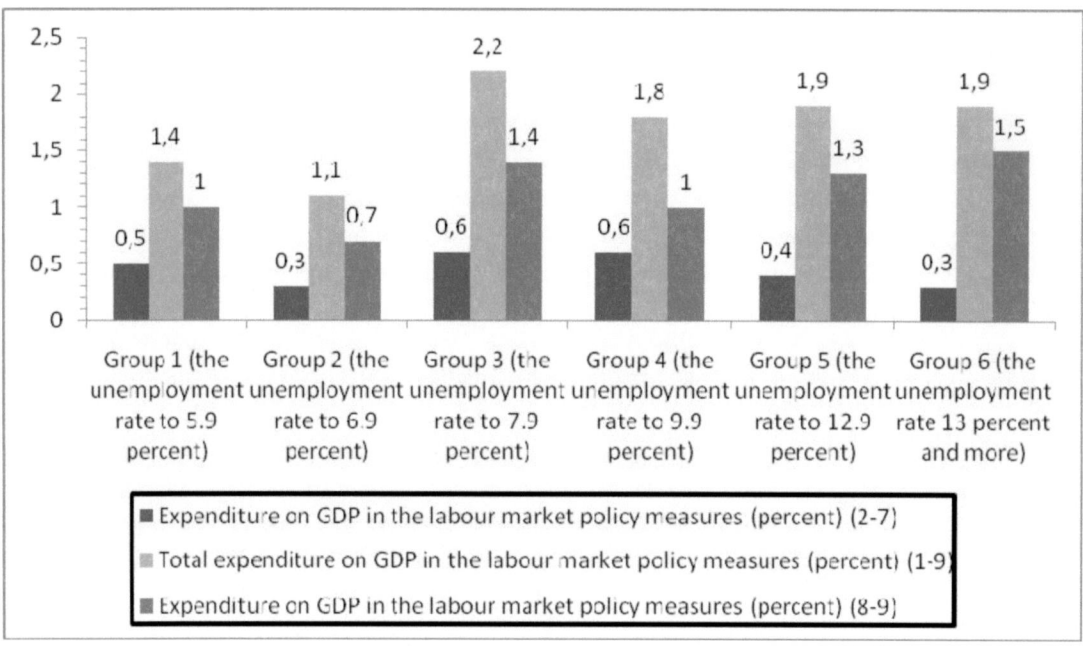

Calculation source: Eurostat.

The Assessment of Opportunities for Different Groups of Inhabitants to Integrate into the Labour Market

An important problem is how to exclude target group of labour market when the situation is being assessed. It should be noted that national statistical offices and Eurostat while doing labour force surveys attribute 15-24 years old people to youth and 55-64 years old people to older people. The latter groups are released by the authors and this paper examines the situation of women and men in the labour market. However, recent focus groups cannot be identified with individuals who are additionally supported in the labour market; the groups of such individuals are distinguished in the national policy level. Law on Support for Employment (15 June 2006 – No X-694 Vilnius) did not divide the groups of the registered in the labour exchange and additionally supported unemployed by gender, but women who are raising and supervising their children can be identified in a large part actually under that provision. On the other hand, discrepancies by gender in individual groups of the unemployed also exist. The latter differences can greatly complicate the assessment of the labour market policy outcomes. The priority was given to the Department of Statistics data in this section of the article in order to avoid these problems.

Employment and Activity Trends of Development

Typically, employment indicators are undeservedly forgotten in the mass media and even in the scientific literature, ignoring the fact that the fundamental cause of real unemployment is a decrease of a number of employed people. Such a one-sided analysis of unemployment can lead to false conclusions about the observed changes in the labour market because the formal unemployment indices tell nothing about the actual causes which determine the dynamics of the number of the unemployed. Assessing the situation in terms of the labour market policy, it is important to take into account the employment and activity rates. The indicators of employment and activity level are perhaps the most appropriate indicators to illustrate disparities of the different target demographic groups in the labour market; specific features of change of indicators will be discussed more largely.

97

Waveform curves are typical of range of employment rate by target demographic groups. This shows a significant effect of the country's economic cycles for different groups in the labour market. Assessing distribution of employment by gender, it is important to note that traditionally employment rates for male are higher than for women (Figure 3). It was especially high among men before the economic crisis in 1998 and 2007 (a little bit more than 60 percent). However, men's employment fell rapidly (especially during the last economic crisis) because an adverse impact of economic cycles fluctuation has asserted.

Observing women's employment, it can be said that the cyclical nature of employment volatility of this demographic group of population is significantly lower than that of men. This is evidenced by significantly lower oscillation amplitude of this rate. In other words, the ups and downs of the female employment rate are much smaller. Therefore, women experienced the less after-effect of the economic crises than men; men have lost far more jobs than the softer sex has lost. Women's employment rate decreased from 54.4 to 50.9 percent in the period of 2007-2010 and this ratio change was felt significantly less than the equivalent men ratio change. Although the youth employment is the lowest, but youth employment after the Russian crisis decreased for a long time significantly faster than that of men and women. Youth employment curve dropped very rapidly when the last economic crisis has started (from 26.7 percent in 2008 to 19.1 percent in 2010). During the period of 2009-2012, only every fifth young person had the work; the similar situation was in those years when Lithuania has joined the EU.

It must be emphasized that, despite the relatively high synchronicity of the development cycles of different demographic groups' employment, the employment trends of elderly differed quite significantly. The wave of older people employment grew almost constantly, but, during the period of 2004-2007, their employment growth was much slower than in other periods when the latter rate was increasing. A significant employment change cycle synchronization of elderly population asserted in 1998-2004 as compared with other demographic groups.

During this period the employment of older people has increased significantly, while variation wave of this index has decreased significantly among other groups of population. It should be admitted that the elderly is the demographic group whose employment has been growing steadily until 2007 almost regardless of the country's economic cycles of development. On the other hand, older people's employment rate dropped from 53.4 percent in 2010 to 48.6 percent in 2007 when the impact of the last economic crisis occurred. However, this negative change was significantly lower as compared with age groups of men and youth. The employment rate of older people was the highest in an unfavourable economic situation in 2008-2009 as compared with other demographic groups of people which were excluded for assessment; this fact proves relatively better situation of older people in the labour market.

Population activity indicator is crucial in terms of labour market policies. The higher the value of the latter index is the more active people of the individual socio-demographic group are in the labour market. The latter index varies considerably less depending on the cyclical nature of economic development, and its analysis cannot actually show some brighter wave-like fluctuations; the analysis of the development trends of employment and unemployment rates shows those fluctuations.

Men's activity was traditionally the highest. It ranged from 7 percentage points in the range (amplitude ranged from 65 to 72 percent). The variation amplitudes of activity level indices of the youth and the elderly are still bigger (the amplitudes fluctuate respectively from 25 to 43 percent and from 43 to 58 percent).

Reverse trends are more typical of activity changes as compared with employment changes in age groups of men and youth. A downward trend in activity asserted more with employment of these groups growing, and activity increased more often with this indicator decreasing. In this way, the activity change of these groups often has the opposite trends in regard to employment changes.

Figure 3. **The Population Employment Rate by the Target Demographic Groups in Lithuania According to Data from Department of Statistics** (percent)*

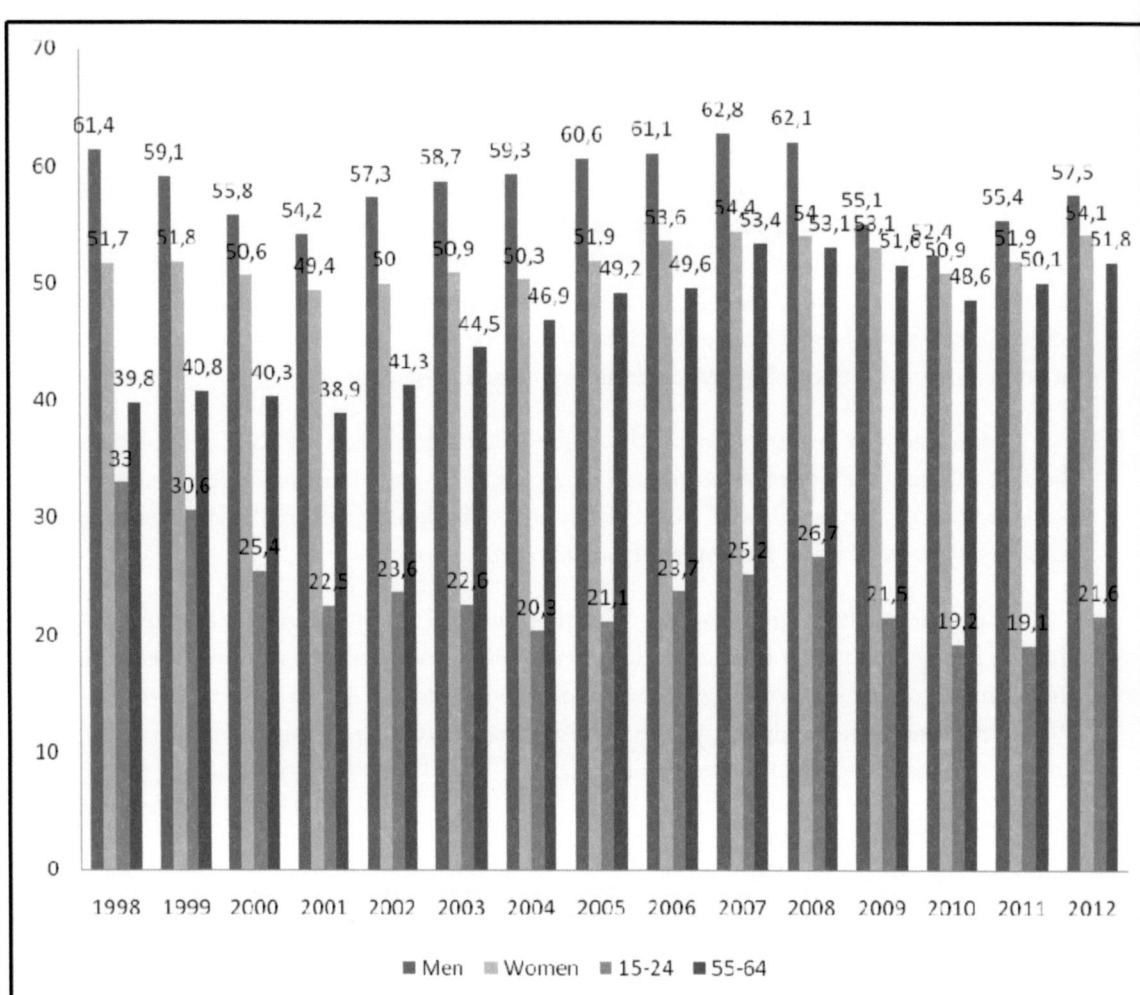

*Employment rate by sex is calculated on the basis of index of 15 years old and the age group of older people.

It is positive that the activity of the elderly in the labour market was almost constantly growing during the period of the analysis. Particularly rapid decline of this rate in the youth age group in 1998-2005 is worrying, but youth activity began to stabilize only after Lithuania's accession to the EU. Significant increase of activity of the elderly in the labour market compensates the increase of inactivity of the young people in the labour market; this situation was observed during the assessment of the situation in the labour market. In 1998, the young and the elderly activity was virtually the same (in round figures it was 43 percent). However, activity of the elderly increased by up to 59 percent up to the year 2012, and youth activity declined to 29 percent, while youth activity in the midst of economic boom in 2006 has been dropped even more (up to 25 percent).

The latter trends can tell us nothing about the causes of the observed changes, but, in fact, there are no studies done in Lithuania which would examine and compare the motivation of the behaviour of different groups in the labour market. Observed trends are overbearing in regard of labour market policy. It is particularly relevant to take into account the observed trends in youth activity, which can be interpreted as a rather passive behaviour of young people in the domestic labour market.

Politicians and experts should pay close attention to formation of the complex measures for active labour market policy which would help the part of the youth to pass from economically inactive to economically active residents. It cannot be limited to the application of active measures by labour exchange. The role of other institutions would be essential to activate youth; these institutions would encourage and assist to economically inactive young people to get good specialities and successfully integrate into the labour market.

Changes of Unemployment

It is important to complement the assessments of labour supply structure with the analysis of the distribution of unemployment level according to the target demographic groups. The latter analysis allows assessing the differences and changes of unemployment level intensity under conditions of the different economic cycles in regard to time.

Wave-like curves are characteristic of unemployment rate fluctuations according to the target demographic groups. A wave of rising unemployment rises when the effect of the country's economic cycles is adverse; the curve of this index fluctuation is falling down when the situation returns to normal.

Traditionally, the rate of youth unemployment is the highest. This can be seen when the situation of demographic groups of the target population in the labour market is compared.

Although youth unemployment increased up to 31.1 percent after the Russian crisis in 2001, but the last economic crisis caused even major growth of youth unemployment in Lithuania (up to 35.1 percent in 2010). The unemployment rate fluctuations of the latter group are highly sensitive to the effects of the economic crisis, and the amplitude of the pending youth unemployment rate fluctuation is the biggest. Unemployment rate of older people was relatively high. The after-effects of the Russian economic crisis were felt a fairly long period of time and these after-effects caused the growth of older people unemployment at the beginning of the nineties. The unemployment rate of the elderly increased from 5.8 to 13.2 percent during the period of 1999-2001. The second wave of the elderly unemployment growth occurred because of the impact of the last economic crisis. Nearly 15 percent economically active older people were out of work in 2010 (Figure 4).

Figure 4. The Unemployment Rate in Lithuania According to the Target Demographic Groups in the Department of Statistics* (percent)

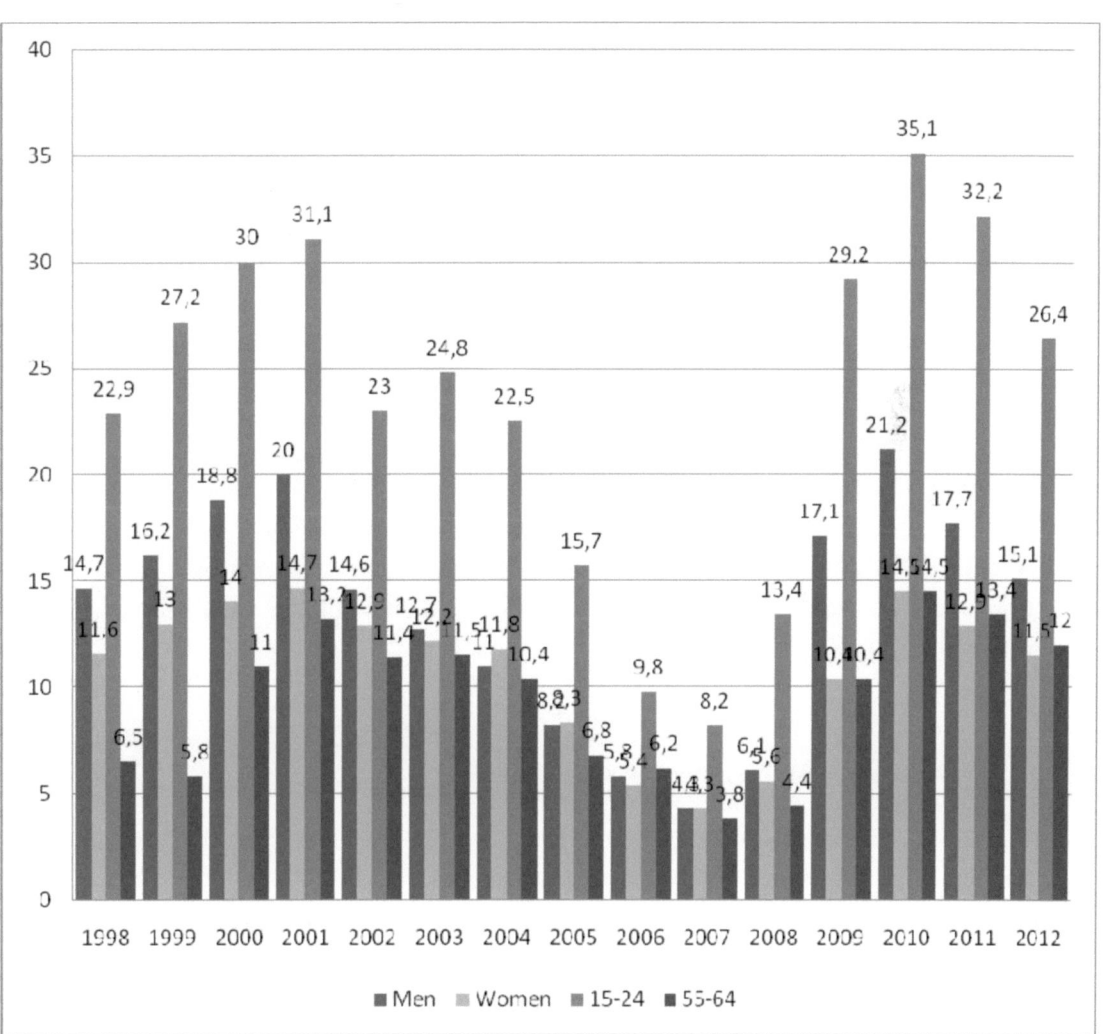

*Unemployment rate by gender is calculated on the basis of the index of 15 years old and older people age group.

Watched changes show very rapid unemployment growth of different demographic groups of the population in Lithuania during the last economic crisis. Despite the fact that the problems of unemployment in Western countries during the crisis have received considerable attention[35], the efforts to maintain and create new jobs have been weak in Lithuania during the economic recession. One can debate about whether there existed a solid job creation policy on the national level in Lithuania during the recent years. Mostly everything was automatically left to business and favourable development of economic cycles; hopefully, the number of workplaces will increase by gravity when the national economy recovers.

The effects of the economic downturns and upswings influence the unemployment differences according to gender. Differences between male and female unemployment usually grow on the impact of the effects of the crisis, but monitored differentiation significantly reduces when the situation returns to normal. In addition, the male unemployment rate fluctuated much faster than the women unemployment rate. The male unemployment rate increased from 4.3 to 21.2 percent, and the female unemployment rate increased from 4.2 to 14.5 percent during the period of 2007-2010. The latter growing trend is explained by "male" job losses during the economic crisis. While male unemployment is usually higher than that of women, but the kind of the latter distribution should not be given too much prominence. A deeper analysis of the observed processes shows that a higher men's activity in the labour market has a significant meaning to their higher unemployment; men's activity in the labour market is much higher than that of women.

Differences in Unemployment by Gender

The analysis of employment and unemployment rates by gender in Lithuania confirms the findings of Emmenegger. Women are more likely to change the position in the labour market than men (observing the so-called "transitions"). Also, Emmenegger believes that women transition from unemployment to employment is more complex than that of men[36]. Human health and social work remained the main area of activity of women in Lithuania; according to the Department of Statistics, almost 68 percent public sector

---

[35]Bertola G. *Labour Market Regulation*. Geneva, ILO (2009).
[36]Emmenegger P. *Gendering Insiders and Outsiders. Labour Market Status and Preferences for Job Security*. Working Papers on the Reconciliation of Work and Welfare in Europe. REC-WP 02 (2010).

employees were women at the end of the last decade. The textile industry, health service and education remain women's "traditional" spheres of employment.

The Regional Changes of Situation in the Labour Market

It is appropriate to establish the differences between urban and rural employment and activity in order to evaluate the situation of the target groups in the labour market. These indicators are important not only to highlight the differentiation fluctuations of the observed indicators, but also to monitor their territorial differences. The analysis of data according to urban and rural characteristics from the latter labour force surveys which were conducted by the Department of Statistics makes much more reliable results than the observed changes in individual counties are evaluated because of the higher whole which covers the population.

The results from the authors' analysis show (Fig. 5) that traditionally higher employment rate in the city testifies to better employment possibilities in the cities (compared to rural). In 2012, urban employment rate was 59.7 percent, rural – 47.4 percent. This suggests that relatively fewer jobs are created for rural people than for urban residents. The existing trends of changes in the level of employment by place of residence during the last economic crisis were similar, but the employment of the rural population was much smaller. Traditionally, rural residents' work in the agricultural sphere ensures their employment. Therefore, the decline of employment in the agrarian sector of the economy determined the dramatic drop in the employment of the rural population in 1997-2010 (almost 10 percent).

Rural employment was almost equal to the urban employment (the latter index values were around 55 percent) during Russia's economic crisis in 1999; rural employment was 12 percent lower in 2012. The latter trend clearly shows the growth of the regional differences in the labour market and increasing employment gap between urban and rural. Another important feature of the development of rural employment is rather limited country's economic growth influence on the dynamics of the number of jobs occupied. For example, the employment of rural population decreased or, in fact, did not even grow in the previous economic upswing (in 2003-2006).

105

It should still be paid attention to the fact that the activity of rural people in the labour market is significantly lower than the activity of urban people (was respectively 65.8 and 52 percent in 2011), and the employment of rural people decreased significantly faster than the employment of urban population during the period in question (1998-2011). This evidences about the relatively lower stimuli of working-age rural people to actively participate in the labour market (to seek employment). It is true to say that the relatively lower activity of the working people in rural areas complicates the opportunities of filling the openings in smaller regions of the country, especially where large proportion of newly established jobs is in the agricultural sphere. The lack of motivation to work generally limits poor opportunities for filling the openings and low activity of the part of population in the labour market. The latter factor clearly asserts in smaller regions of the country.

It is worrying that jobs for rural people in Lithuania were created especially few. This resulted in a high relative unemployment of rural people. This rate increased particularly rapidly during the last economic crisis when this rate reached a record high. Unemployment rate in rural areas in 2010-2011 even exceeded 20 percent limit according to labour force surveys. Much higher unemployment rate values indicate that the integration of rural people into the labour market during the crisis worsened more than the integration of the urban population. The relatively low economic activity of rural population is becoming a serious obstacle to the integration of unemployed people from agrarian (rural) regions of the country into the labour market.

The long-term unemployment has increased during the economic downturn. One of the worst effects of the economic downturn is its long-term effect which has been evidenced over the growth of the number of the unemployed who are unable to find work for more than a year. The country's labour market has experienced two large-scale shocks – the Russian crisis and the latter global economic crisis. According to the Department of Statistics data analysis on long-term unemployment, it is noted that long-term unemployment rate has reached its peak after two – three years after the start of the economic downturn.

According to the analysis of the duration of unemployment of different age groups of the unemployed, it can be maintained that older than 50 years old people are the most vulnerable in respect of long-term unemployment. According to the data of the Department of Statistics, the part of the older unemployed who were unable to find work for more than 12 months has exceeded 60 percent for a long period of recovery after the economic downturn in 1998; although the part of the long-term unemployed in the total population was about 40 percent.

Another outstanding problem of the long-term unemployed is its very bright territorial shade. In recent years, the increase of rural people's long-term unemployment surprises. It is noted that the number of the long-term unemployed much depends especially on the cyclical nature of the country's economic development. Long-term unemployment of rural population particularly rapidly grew under the influence of the last economic crisis. The level of the latter index in rural areas has increased from 1.5 to 11.8 percent in the period of 2008-2011, while it grew much slower in the cities (from 1.1 to 6.3 percent).

The differences in the evolution of the observed changes are characterized by the movement of "centre of gravity" of the long-term unemployment from the city to the countryside in the last years of economic boom in 2006-2007; the latter indicator became higher in the rural areas than in the urban areas during the entire period of 2006-2011. It must be emphasized that by 2005 both long-term and the general level of unemployment rate in urban areas was higher than in rural areas, but later the trends of this index change have changed in an unfavourable direction for the rural population. A large proportion of working-age people in rural areas fell into "the trap of long-term unemployment" because of a lack of jobs and motivation to work. It is believed that the extremely slow economic and social development of smaller regions of the country discourages the creation of jobs and business and forms this situation.

It seems that the long-term unemployment in rural areas in Lithuania can really become a "chronic" disease. Prolonged long-term unemployment in rural areas asserted in the fact that the growth of this rate has continued even in 2011, when the Lithuanian economy has pretty much recovered. It should be stated that prolonged long-term unemployment in rural regions significantly complicates the opportunities of socio-economic growth in rural regions. The latter group of labour resources quasi stays away from positive social and economic changes.

Statistical data from labour exchange show that the problem of unemployment in different regions of the country is extremely difficult. Therefore, unemployment can be identified as a relevant regional problem. For example, painful effects of past economic crisis are still felt and these effects caused high relative unemployment rate in districts of Ignalina, Zarasai and Anykščiai in 2011. According to data from labour exchange, extremely high value of this index was in Ignalina district in 2010 (21.2 percent). The latter areas are attributable to depressive regions of the country according to the current situation in these regions. Depressed regions in terms of the labour market are defined as the main target areas because of employment and unemployment problems which remain the longest in these regions.[37]

On the other hand, the difference between the highest and the lowest unemployment rate was about 4 times in municipal level in 2010-2011. This suggests that different areas have very different employment and social development potential in terms of the development of human resources which create surplus value. The unfavourable wage differentiation complicates better social and economic development opportunities of smaller regions of the country. This problem is not new traditionally. Big labour payment discrepancies were observed in the country at the beginning of the last decade.[38]

---

[37]Andriušaitienė D. *Depresinių šalies regionų darbo rinkos plėtra*. Vilnius, Lithuanian Labour Market Training Authority (2008).
[38]*Tūkstantmečio plėtros tikslai: Lietuvos regionų vystymosi analizė*. Vilnius, United Nations (2004 p. 31-32).

Figure 5. **Long-term Unemployment Rate of Urban and Rural Residents in Lithuania according to the Data of the Department of Statistics** (in percent)

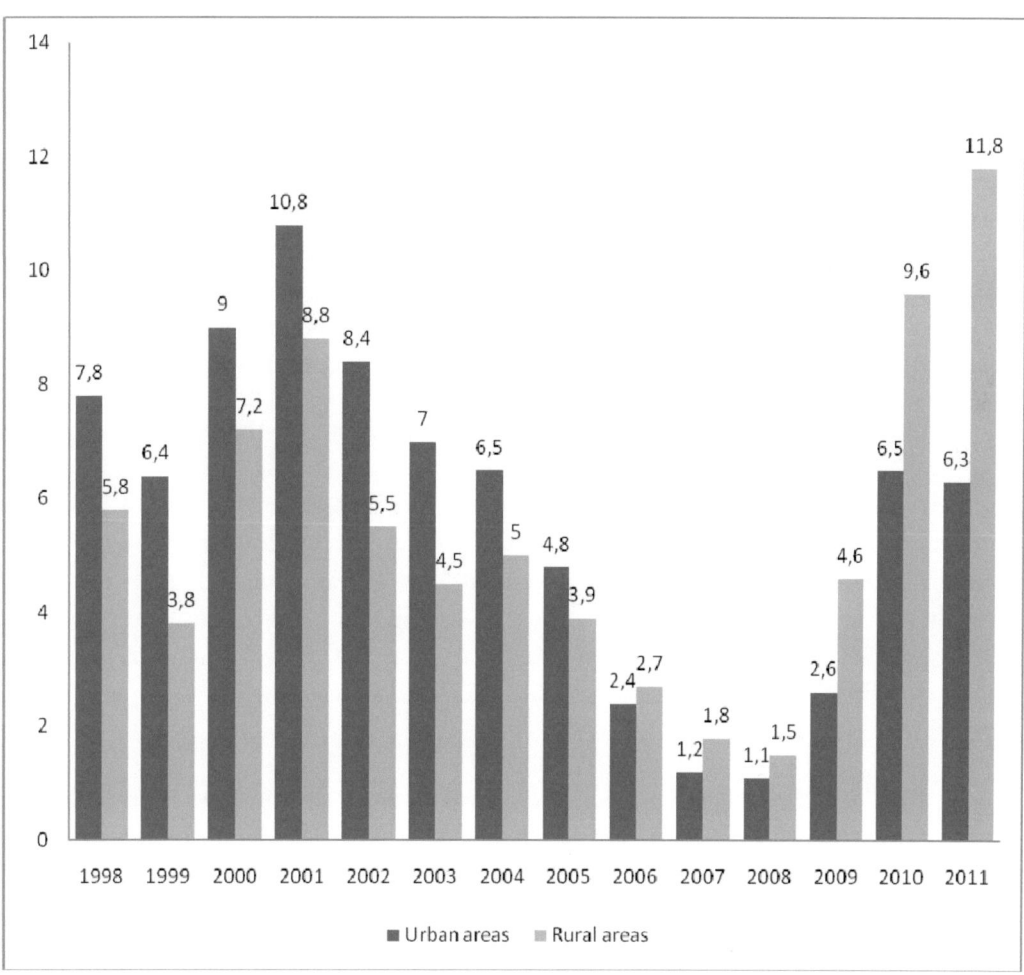

Conclusions

Despite the negative trends of the economic crisis in Lithuania, employment rate of men remained the highest when comparing different demographic groups. Women's employment has always been lower, although it is high enough in Lithuania to EU extent. In addition, they are far better adapted to the consequences of the most recent economic crisis than men. Therefore, common quantitative indices of women's employment and unemployment actually more conceal than reflect the problems of women in the labour market. Women in Lithuania especially lack jobs of high quality which would provide higher wages; flexible forms of employment are not common in the country. The latter forms of employment would allow the better use of their potential in the labour market.

On the whole, the development trends of older people in the labour market were favourable. However, older people find it difficult to find work in smaller regions of the country and in rural areas where the risk of long-term unemployment has increased. More incentives should be used for both older people and women to hold down in the labour market by increasing their activity. Adverse employment and activity trends for young people are especially worrying, but when encouraging them to integrate into the labour market at the same time it should be avoided employment decline among older people. This would help to avoid the negative effect of displacement of the older people from the labour market.

Results of the analysis revealed weaknesses in the country's labour market. To sum up the situation it can be suggested that much more attention should be given to rural people in pursuance of the active labour market policies. It is believed that the involvement of youth and rural working-age people into active measures should become the underlying direction of the labour market policy implementation. The analysis of situation differences between urban and rural position in the labour market should be added to the assessment in the individual areas level; these differences reflect the specificity of the situation in areas of high-unemployment.

Positive effect in terms of population activity occurs when the unemployed, even in the case of unsuccessful placement, will continue to actively integrate into the labour market again looking for a job or participating in active measures. Inactive population falls out of the labour market and becomes large load of the country's welfare state system. It must be emphasized that highly different trends of the population and the unemployed activity which were found during the study show the relatively low systemic social policy effectiveness in Lithuania (the gap between the population and the unemployed activity rates was very high during their participation in active measures according to the data from conducted estimates by Labour and Social Research Institute). Therefore, the conclusion is that the activity of the unemployed may have little impact on the total population activity. It is believed that active measures should become an important condition for social benefits pay for unemployed people of working age. This would encourage the integration of problematic population groups into the labour market.

In conclusion, it should be noted that labour market policy measures which are applied in Lithuania have a positive impact on the total employment of the population, and especially on representatives of population groups which are more difficult to integrate into the labour market (young people, the disabled, senior citizens and so on). However, ALMPM funding decreased significantly (especially in respect of the total number of unemployed) after the economic downturn in 2008-2009, therefore, involvement of the registered unemployed in ALMPM respectively decreased. Vocational training programs and employment by subsidizing funding fell most according to the measures. Women and older residents' participation fell most according to groups of unemployed.

Through innovation in the field of labour market policy, it is appropriate to increase the variety of measures and their conformity with the opportunities of the integration of the unemployed in the labour market. On the one hand, it is necessary to increase the mobility of services and the unemployed to ensure greater access to ALMPM. On the other hand, it is necessary to strengthen the formation of the motivation for the work in general education system, because lack of motivation for work reduces even the most attractive ALMPM performance. At the same time, compatibility of labour market measures with the social support policy measures and the execution of the overall social and economic policies in the municipalities should be increased. The integrity of the labour market policy with the overall country's economic policy should be constantly increased.

It is necessary to increase the mobility of services, and to focus on the unemployed mobility (especially in rural areas where the unemployed are often isolated from opportunities to participate in ALMPM) in developing of innovation in ALMPM

111

implementation. More attention should be paid to work with young people in comprehensive schools. Labour and Social Research Institute studies have shown[39] that a large part of youth unemployment is caused by lack of work motivation, which has not been formed in comprehensive school grades 6-10.

Having no motivation to work, young people sluggishly choose the professional career path, randomly choose vocational training institutions, or do not choose at all and as a result about 50 percent unemployed young people, who are registered in Lithuanian Labour Exchange (employment service), have no professional readiness. So, another innovation of the improvement of the labour market policy direction is the education of work motivation in comprehensive schools. Particular attention should be paid to young people from social risk families, because studies have shown that the youth from those social strata mostly have the lowest work motivation and are more exposed to the problems in the labour market.

---

[39]Gruževskis B., Zabarauskaitė R., Martinaitis Ž., Pocius, A., Biveinytė S. Factors of a Successful Career in the Labour Market. Ministry of Education and Science. Labour and Social Research Institute. Vilnius, 2007.

List of References

Academic Publications and Researches

1. Andriušaitienė D. *Depresinių šalies regionų darbo rinkos plėtra*. Vilnius, Lietuvos darbo rinkos mokymo tarnyba (2008).
2. Barro R.J. *Macroeconomics*. Fourth Edition. John Wiley and Sons, Inc. New York (1993, p.145-162).
3. Bertola G. *Labour Market Regulation*. Geneva, ILO (2009).
4. Emmenegger P. *Gendering Insiders and Outsiders. Labour Market Status and Preferences for Job Security*.Working Papers on the Reconciliation of Work and Welfare in Europe. REC-WP 02 (2010).
5. Gruževskis B., Kabaila A., Moskvina J., Okunevičiūtė Neverauskienė L. *Bedarbių užimtumo rėmimas. Užimtumo rėmimo programų efektyvumo vertinimas*. Vilnius, Darbo ir socialinių tyrimų institutas (2006).
6. Gruževskis B., Zabarauskaitė R., Martinaitis Ž., Pocius A. Biveinytė S. *Sėkmingos karjeros darbo rinkoje veiksniai*. Vilnius, Švietimo ir mokslo ministerija, Darbo ir socialinių tyrimų institutas (2007).
7. Moskvina J, Okunevičiūtė Neverauskienė L. *Aktyvi darbo rinkos politika: teorija ir praktika*. Vilnius, Vilniaus Gedimino technikos universitetas (2011, p.52).
8. Okunevičiūtė Neverauskienė L., Moskvina J. *Aktyvios darbo rinkos politikos priemonių socialinė nauda*. Filosofija. Sociologija. Vilnius (2010, p.101-111).
9. *The Global Competitiveness Report 2013-2014*. Word Economic Forum (2013). Available at: http://reports.weforum.org/the-global-competitiveness-report-2013-2014/.
10. *Tūkstantmečio plėtros tikslai: Lietuvos regionų vystymosi analizė*. Vilnius, Jungtinės tautos (2004, p. 31-32.).

Other Sources of Information

11. *Apskrito stalo diskusija Europos Komisijos atstovybėje Lietuvoje*. Vilnius (2013 09 04).
12. Gruževskis, B.; Kabaila, A.; Bagdžiūnienė, D.; Okunevičiūtė Neverauskienė, L. *Bedarbių profesinio mokymo naudos tyrimas, įvertinant mokymo programų vykdymo efektyvumą bei*

praktinio mokymo kokybę. Mokslinio tyrimo ataskaita. Darbo ir socialinių tyrimų institutas, Vilnius (2006).

13. 2002-2012 m. Darbo ir socialinių tyrimų instituto atliktų įvairių tyrimų apklausos.
14. Lietuvos Respublikos užimtumo rėmimo įstatymas (2006 m. birželio 15 d. nr. x-694, Vilnius).
15. Darbo biržos duomenys bei skelbiama informacija (ttp://www.ldb.lt/Informacija/Puslapiai/default.aspx).
16. Statistikos departamento duomenys bei skelbiama informacija (http://www.stat.gov.lt/).
17. http://db1.stat.gov.lt/statbank/default.asp?w=1920.

The new meaning of innovation in the contect of structural changes of economy

Dr. oec. Tatjana Volkova, BA School of Business and Finance

Inta Baranovska, National Centre for Education

The aim of this paper is to identify the problems arising due to structural changes in economy, thus broadening the meaning of innovations. For business managers it is vital to understand the essence of technological and non-technological innovations and their role in creating product value for the company, appreciate interconnectedness, and identify development trends to ensure efficient and effective innovation management by a broader involvement of women and the elderly in business activities. Economy is driven by changing and diverse needs of customers. It leads to structural changes in economy. Due to the industrial revolution, during the last centuries the production sector was the dominating sector of economy, while nowadays the biggest part of the GDP is contributed by the service sector. It is influenced by an increasing level of customer welfare and hence a growing demand for diverse services. There is also a growing demand for services in production and the business to business sector (B2B). Production companies use software, logistics, design, telecommunications, finance, after sales and other services to a greater extent in order to increase the market value of products and productivity under ever tougher competitive conditions. Integration of services in the value chain process of production companies is an integral part of the activities of a company. The changing structure of economy and increased competition imply a need for companies to move from simplified products to more sophisticated processes and products, aiming to deliver higher added value in comparison with the average in the industry, thus leading to a competitive advantage. Such companies are less influenced by economy and industrial life cycles and prices of production inputs. The current changes determine the necessity of a new type of thinking and new approaches to conducting business, ability to learn from past experiences, at the same time being aware of local and global challenges for the company, the state, the region, when facing new risks and opportunities. Taking into account that companies and industries are not monolith, there exist diverse innovation strategies and types of innovations used by companies.

Key words: *technological innovations, non-technological innovations, innovation strategies*

Introduction

Europe needs innovations in all sectors of economy and society to achieve economic development. In order to ensure recovery of economy, politicians of many countries search for new approaches to economic management, develop reform and stabilisation plans, while entrepreneurs and the public often criticise these plans and demand immediate solutions and support; they expect more constructive actions from the government. Unfortunately, the solutions and the gained experience that were of use yesterday can no longer be valid today due to the rapid changes of the surrounding environment, for the swift development of modern technologies and globalisation offer an increasing number of new opportunities how to address the needs, at the same time creating new necessities.

The term 'innovation economy' should not be understood only as innovative companies or products. Both of these concepts are of course connected, but are far from being synonymous. Innovation economy can be described as economy that is driven by innovations in their broadest sense of the word, functioning to enhance the quality of life in society. To achieve this, an innovative environment needs to be created, which entails the creation of open and excellent research systems, availability of venture capital, human resources and intellectual capital development etc. In the research carried out by the European Commission on Innovative Performance in the EU *("Innovation Union Scoreboard", 2013)*, that evaluates the landscape of innovation in all the 27 member states, Latvia was ranked 25, which is among the last places in the EU scoreboard *(Innovation Scoreboard, 2013, p.7)*[40].

Currently the Ministry of Economy of Latvia mentions the capacity-building of research potential as well as insufficient financial resources allocated for Research and Development (R&D) as the main challenges that hamper the development of the National Innovation System. In 2011 allocations for R&D constituted only 0.7% of the GDP, whereas the average level in the EU was 2% in 2010. Latvia also shows low innovation capacity in the private sector, a low level of commercialisation of R&D results, and insufficient cooperation between science and business sectors. Another problem is a lack

---

[40] Innovation Union Scoreboard.Available at: http://ec.europa.eu/enterprise/policies/innovation/facts-figures-analysis/innovation-scoreboard/index_en.htm

of qualified specialists to enable companies, scientific institutions to develop and launch innovative projects, create new technologies or products. Latvia has a relatively high proportion of low and medium-low technology sectors; during the period of 2008-2010 the percentage of innovative companies constituted 29.9% of the total number of businesses in Latvia; in the EU it was 51.6% on the average during 2006-2008; in Lithuania – 30.3%, while in Estonia – 56.4%. Business people still lack understanding of the role of innovations to boost competiveness (Platace, 2013)[41]. Companies fail to realize the full innovative potential of human resources, as there are untapped potential for women entrepreneurship and women leadership.The main reason - leadership either doesn't know how to foster their insights or lacks the perspective necessary to endorse women ideas;

Research methodology

The following research methods have been used: general theoretical methods, content analysis, trend analysis, as well as data analysis methods.

Research findings

STRUCTURAL CHANGES IN ECONOMY AND A CHANGE IN THE IMPORTANCE OF PRODUCTION

Over the last decades significant changes can be observed in the proportion of services and manufacturing sectors in the economy of developed countries; this illustrates the trend that the services sector has been becoming increasingly more important for employment and added value.

---

[41]Platace L. Neinovatīvā Latvija. Kā veicināt Latvijas konkurētspēju. Available at: http://www.lvportals.lv/print.php?id=252340

McKinsey Global Institute has carried out research on the role of manufacturing in the economy of developed and developing countries, in order to find out what the opportunities for various industries are to ensure most efficient functioning. The research findings illustrate the following trends: manufacturing has a significant role in both, developed and also developing countries, the manufacturing sector is diverse and it incorporates increasing number of services in its operation processes and uses those as input resources. The research also reveals the importance of the production sector in creation of workplaces changes in the next stage of economic development. The production sector provides essential contribution to the development of the trade sector, provision of expenditure for R&D, and the growth of productivity. The production sector also ensures 70% of export in the economy of developed and also developing countries and almost 90% of R&D expenditure *(Manyka J et al., 2013: 17)*[42]. In the future, the manufacturing sector will also continue to promote innovations, export and productivity.

Productivity can be raised by reducing the number of employees or increasing productivity. Due to globalisation and emergence of new technologies, competition increases resulting in the fall of average costs in many industries, which forces the enterprises to exercise measures to decrease costs in order to ensure competiveness and the necessary level of profit for development. Unfortunately, the enterprises that focus on decreasing costs in order to increase productivity under the influence of growing competition are forced to diminish the number of employees by replacing them with modern technologies. More and more companies in Europe and elsewhere in the world cut the number of employees due to the crisis and also the intensification of global competition, as companies are forced to compete on the global scale, and therefore the reduction of costs is critical. For instance, the world leader in the production of industrial ball-bearings the Swedish company SKF announced at the beginning of 2013 that it would cut 2500 workplaces. This reduction of workplaces was part of measures included in the austerity programme of 2010. It was announced that employees would be made redundant not only in SKF subsidiaries in Sweden but also in Italy, Ukraine, and the USA. The SKF announcement states that the employees will take early retirement, choose voluntary

---

[42] Manyka J et al.Manufacturing the future: the next era of global growth and Innovation, McKinsey Global Institute, McKinsey Operations Practise, November 2012. p. 17. Tiešsaiste (skatīts 21.03.2013.). Available at:http://www.mckinsey.com/insights/manufacturing/the_future_of_manufacturing

redundancy or the dismissal will be negotiated with their labour unions. SKF profit has been decreasing lately, therefore austerity measures are taken[43].

The Japanese car manufacturer 'Honda' also announced at the beginning of 2013 that it would dismiss 800 workers at the UK plant in Swindon, resulting in more than 25% decrease in the number of employees at the plant. In the 'Honda' announcement it was stated that such a decision had been made in order to ensure "long-term stability of the business", as the demand in the European car market, where the plant's production was realised, was not high at the time. At present there are around 3500 employees at the Swindon plant[44].

At the end of 2012 the German light fixture producer 'Osram' announced that in order to diminish the expenses and be more competitive with Asian companies, they will dismiss about 4700 or 12% or all their 39 000 employees and will close or sell several plants. Dismissals are part of billion EUR worth austerity measure programme that will be implemented in the next three years. Earlier the company had already notified that until 2014 they plan to liquidate at least 7 300 jobs. At the same time 'Osram' has intended to open a new Light Emitting Diode (LED) plant in China with 1 700 jobs by 2017. Lately the competiveness of 'Osram' has been declining because the manufacturer is slow to reorient production from conventional incandescent bulbs to energy-saving LED bulbs instead. Meanwhile the LED bulb manufacturers in Asia have significantly increased their production capacity and have lowered the prices of these light fixtures. At present 'Osram' is owned by the production giant 'Siemens', while in the near future it plans to secede

---

[43]Pasaulē lielākais industriālo lodīšu gultņu ražotājs SKF samazinās 2500 darbavietas. 14.01.13. [Retrieved: 11.02.2013.] Available at:http://news.lv/BNS/2013/01/14/Pasaule-lielakais-industrialo-lodisu-gultnu-razotajs-SKF-samazinas-2500-darbavietas
[44]"Honda" Lielbritānijas rūpnīcā atlaidīs 800 darbinieku. 11.01.13. [Retrieved: 11.02.2013.]Available at:http://news.lv/BNS/2013/01/11/Honda-Lielbritanijas-rupnica-atlaidis-800-darbinieku.

from the parent company.[45]Research conducted in Sweden indicates that 25% of the companies hold a strong opinion that job cuts will also be among top priorities in 2013[46].

Similar situation can also be observed in many companies in Latvia, when as a result of changes in demand and under the pressure of the necessity to diminish costs, they are forced to dismiss employees which causes social tensions. The redundancies are one of the ways that increases productivity of the company. For example, in 2012 JSC airBaltic decreased the number of its employers by 15% (Melbārzde L., 2013)[47]. Due to the reduction of demand 'Liepājas Metalurgs' has notified that in April 2013 it will decrease the number of available jobs and terminate employment relationships on the grounds of mutual agreement. 80 jobs will be cut, saving 49.6 thousand LVL per month. Even now it is still planned and discussed to cut 229 more jobs. JSC 'Liepājas Metalurgs' states that steel producers are facing similar problems everywhere in the world, as, for example, *ArcelorMittal S.A* that is based in Luxembourg has announced that will close 7 out of 12 plants in Belgium, Liege and 1300 people will lose their jobs. The German biggest steel manufacturer *Thyssen Krupp* faced the losses of 4.7 billion EUR last year (Ž. Hāka, 2013)[48].

The given examples show that the productivity of companies that are based on low costs will dismiss employees in order to increase productivity. This mainly applies to enterprises that are forced to replace their staff by the latest technologies in order to reduce costs, thus replacing human physical and mental potential.

In the developed countries we see a rise in employment in the production sector which follows a fall in the volume of production as the result of the economic crises. However,

---

[45]Lai samazinātu tēriņus, "Osram" likvidēs 4700 darbavietu un slēgs ražotnes.BNS. 30.11.2012.] . Available at: www.mansbizness.lv

[46] Ceturtā daļa firmu plāno samazināt darbinieku skaitu. [Retrieved: 05.05.13.]Available at: http://www.kasjauns.lv/lv/zinas/106694/ceturtdala-zviedrijas-firmu-plano-samazinat-darbinieku-skaitu, 2013

[47] Melbārzde L. Airbaltic cirps darbinieku skaitu un samazinās biļešu cenas. [Retrieved: 05.05.2013.]Available at: http://www.db.lv/razosana/transports-logistika/airbaltic-cirps-darbinieku-skaitu-un-samazinas-bilesu-cenas-253016

[48]Hāka Ž. Liepājas metalurgs atlaidīs darbiniekus un samazinās algas. [Retrieved: 05.05.2013.]Available at: http://www.db.lv/finanses/investors/papildinata-liepajas-metalurgs-atlaidis-darbiniekus-un-samazinas-algas-392410

the sustainability of this trend depends on a number of factors (*Manyka J et al., 2013, pp. 53-55*)[49]:

1. availability of cheap labour force or highly qualified (or both);
2. distance from end consumers;
3. efficiency of transportation and the logistics system;
4. availability of natural resources and cheap electric power;
5. availability of services of innovation centres.

When economy develops, the manufacturing sector still plays an important role in creation of innovations that solve common problems in society: reduction of environmental impact, reduction in the use of recourses and other, a growth in productivity and promotion of trade. However, in the long-term the role of production companies in promotion of employment will diminish in the developed countries due to:

- productivity growth,
- increase in the proportion of the service sector in the GDP and
- intensification of global competition.

Developed countries cannot expect the manufacturing sector to ensure mass employment as it was the case a few decades ago. When analysing opportunities to create new jobs that would result in an increased level of quality of life of the people, it is important to acknowledge the growing role of the service sector in increasing employment. New technologies create new needs and thus a demand for information and its processing, as the internet provides new opportunities, for example, "The Internet of Things (IoT)" currently developed by "Ericsson", provides new experiences for consumers, for example, creating an opportunity for house owners to remotely manage various electronic devices and thus creates a high demand for services of the software industry.

---

[49] Manyka J et al.Manufacturing the future: the next era of global growth and Innovation, McKinsey Global Insitute, McKinsey Operations Practise, November 2012, 53-55. [Retrieved: 21.03.2013.]Available at: http://www.mckinsey.com/insights/manufacturing/the_future_of_manufacturing

The term 'Industry' is increasingly used more often, though not always truly understanding its meaning. Industry is formed by companies that offer their products (goods and services) in the market in order to meet the specific needs of the consumer. For example, software industry addresses the needs for programming services, the advertisement industry takes care of advertising services, coffee industry satisfies the demand for coffee, watch industry takes care of demand for watches, etc.

In this way an industry is formed by companies delivering to the market similar products that meet the same needs of consumers. For instance, the soft drink industry is made from lemonade, kvass, coca-cola, pepsi-cola and other drinks, addressing the consumers' needs for soft drinks.

At the same time it is crucially important not only to acknowledge the needs of today but even more so to define or create the needs that will have to be addressed in the future. We are witnessing the birth of many new industries that are accompanied by a development of modern technologies. For example, the GPS industry could not exist before the invention of the internet and the same applies to digital glasses industry which is still only being formed. Hence, in each country the political leaders have to plan development not only by taking into account the economy sectors development trends, but also making a thorough study of consumers' needs on industry level. Namely, it is necessary to analyse the trends of development in society and determine which needs grow more rapidly and what ecosystem needs to be created, in order to facilitate the growth of the respective industries. For instance, nowadays the production of goods is impossible without the services of design industry , software, advertising, music industry and other services. In economy everything is interconnected and therefore one industry cannot be singled out among the others. At present it is crucial for companies to collaborate, creating clusters that aim at specific end product or solution of a problem. E.g., in Finland such a cluster works not only on industry level, but also on problems level. The aging cluster is created aiming to solve issues caused by the ageing of population in Finland.

Manufacturers become wiser by outsourcing on the global level and thus increasing the demand for highly qualified employees globally. According to the data provided by McKinsey Global Institute, if the current trends remain constant, employment in the manufacturing sector will decrease and jobs will be reduced from the current 45 million to 40 million by 2030 (*Manyka J et al., 2013: 8*) in the economy of developed countries.

In this research it was also emphasised that manufacturers can no longer use traditional approaches. The same applies to economic policy makers who have to meet their own expectations as policies can no longer be shaped by the misconception that production will ensure mass employment. Instead, production entities become a driving force for innovations and state competitiveness. Innovations in production process, materials, IT and others make production opportunities available for a wider number of participants. This refers to first and foremost, the creation of prototypes in the digital environment, possibilities to order mass production of the goods, virtually using the so-called shared production facilities that are based on an open innovation approach. For instance, the first shared production facility in China was opened in 2010, but already in 2011 the Shanghai municipality publicly announced their plans to open 100 such government funded production facilities. Such factories also develop in several USA cities *(Manyka J et al., 2013: 95)*[50]. The internet provides opportunities to use such websites as *Kikcstarter* and *Quirky*, so that everyone could hand in their start-up ideas, for whose realisation external funding can be raised. Virtual economy fosters the demand for production in growing and advanced economies, continuing the process of merging of production and services. Adoption to the needs of people creates production and services innovations that became available due to opportunities provided by digital environments. For instance, the USA expects the demand for personal medical services to increase by 11% each year, reaching 450 billion USD in 2015 *(Manyka J et al., 2013: 100)*[51].

DIVERSITY OF THE PRODUCTION SECTOR

The research carried out by MsKinsley *(Manyka J et al., 2013, pp. 44-45)* [52] deserves a mention as it reveals that the manufacturing sector is not homogenous. In this research,

---

[50] Op. cit., p. 95.

[51] Manyka J et al.Manufacturing the future: the next era of global growth and Innovation, McKinsey Global Institute, McKinsey Operations Practise, November 2012. p. 100. [Retrieved: 21.03.2013.]. Available at: http://www.mckinsey.com/insights/manufacturing/the_future_of_manufacturing

[52] Manyka J et al.Manufacturing the future: the next era of global growth and Innovation, McKinsey Global Institute, McKinsey Operations Practise, November 2012. pp. 44.-45. [Retrieved: 21.03.2013.]. Available at: http://www.mckinsey.com/insights/manufacturing/the_future_of_manufacturing

five different production sectors have been singled out according to the following indicators:

1. sources of advantages in competition;
2. factors influencing the location of production facilities;
3. provision of R&D;
4. expansion of market outlets.

According to the above mentioned indicators, 4 production sectors can be established:

1. **Global innovations for local markets** that consists of the chemical and pharmaceutical sector, production of transportation equipment, machinery, including electrical machinery and appliances. Competitiveness is based on innovation and quality, as well as high R&D costs.

2. **Regional processing** includes printing and publishing, production of food and beverages, rubber and plastics, production of metals articles. The companies in this sector usually have relatively low expenditure for R&D and high automation. The driving force for development is demand in the local market.

3. **The sector of energy and resource intensive production of consumer goods** consists of production of wood products, paper and pulp, metal production, mineral products. The companies that form this sector can be characterised by price competition and a low level of differentiation.

4. **Global technologies** consist of production of computers and office equipment, semiconductors and electronics, medical, precision and optical equipment. Companies in this sector base their competiveness on high investments in R&D and the use of cutting-edge technologies.

5. **Labour intensive sector** consists of production of textiles, clothing, leather, furniture, jewellery, toys and other mainstream commodities. Competition is based on price competition (*Manyka J et al., 2013: 45*)[53].

---

[53] Op. cit., p. 45.

The significance of different factors, such as labour costs, availability of talents, proximity of the market, such partners as suppliers and researchers changes in various sectors of economy. This kind of segmentation of production companies helps to understand where production activities will take place and what role innovations will play in different production sectors.

Production sector developmenttrends

When describing the trends that will influence the production process and design of production digital platforms in the future, *McKinsey* Global Institute states that digital modelling, simulation, and visualisation as well as advances in industrial robotics, additive manufacturing and green production will have a significant impact on the work of manufacturing companies.

1. **Digital modelling, simulation and visualisation**. A digital factory as a model of the entire manufacturing process. Manufacturers can use big data analysis to be able to manage complex production processes and value chains that involve hundreds of suppliers around the world. Toyota, Nissan and Fiat have decreased the expenditure of production of new cars from 30% up to 50%, by using digital chains and therefore allowing manufacturers and designers to share information, simulate the design in order to test the best designs and choose the necessary materials and suppliers (*Manyka J et al., 2013: 88*)[54];

2. **Use of industrial robotics**. At the end of 2010 an estimated one billion industrial robots were used worldwide, mostly in production of cars and electronics. Industrial robots are mostly used in economies where the labour force is highly educated and the costs are high. It is estimated that by 2016 the number of industrial robots will grow by 26% each year, bringing robots to new regions and industries (*Manyka J et al., 2013: 95*)[55];

---

[54] Op. cit., p. 88.

[55] Manyka J et al.Manufacturing the future: the next era of global growth and Innovation, McKinsey Global Institute, McKinsey Operations Practise, November 2012, 95 p. [Retrieved: 21.03.2013.]. Available at: http://www.mckinsey.com/insights/manufacturing/the_future_of_manufacturing

3. Additive manufacturing refers to manufacturing that is based on small particles, for example, 3D printer allows building up a bicycle from synthetic materials. Selective laser sintering, fused deposition modelling, stereo lithography are all key technologies for additive manufacturing. The above technologies mentioned foster flexibility of production by cutting prototyping and development time, reducing material waste, enabling production of complex shapes and structures and offer other advantages.

4. Green production. The use of new technologies and materials can decrease the negative footprint in nature.

Only two out of five segments – regional processing industries (rubber and plastic products, metal products, food, beverages, tobacco, printing and publishing), global innovations for local markets industries (production of chemicals, cars, machinery and appliances) – constitute up to 75% of the added value in manufacturing in both developed and developing countries. Two other production sectors – global technologies (production of computers and office equipment, semiconductors and electronics, medical, precision and optical equipment) and labour intensive consumer goods (production of textiles, clothes, leather, furniture, jewellery, toys and other mainstream commodities) – make up only 16% of added value in manufacturing companies in both developed and developing countries (*Manyka J., et al., 2013: 6*)[56].

The developed countries retain the leading role in global innovations for the local markets with a higher added value; they are less competitive in the labour intensive group. This determines the need for the developed countries to specialise in high-tech sectors, whose development is promoted by state and private sector investments in R&D.

---

[56]Manyka J et al.Manufacturing the future: the next era of global growth and Innovation, McKinsey Global Institute, McKinsey Operations Practise, November 2012., 6 p. [Retrieved: 21.03.2013.]. Available at: http://www.mckinsey.com/insights/manufacturing/the_future_of_manufacturing

THE GROWING SIGNIFICANCE OF SERVICES IN ECONOMY

The research carried out by the Global Company MsKinsey claims that the manufacturing sector reaches its maximum when it makes up to 20-35% of the GDP. When the level of development in the country increases, a more rapid demand in the services sector emerges, creating a decrease in employment in manufacturing. For example, in the USA the proportion of employment in the manufacturing sector decreased from 25% in 1950 to 9% in 2008. A similar situation can be observed in this sector in Germany: if in 1970 the manufacturing employment share formed 35% of the GDP, in 2008 it was only 18% (*Manyka J et al., 2013: 3*)[57].

All in all over the last 10 years, employment in the manufacturing sector in advanced economies has dropped by 19% from 63 million in 1998 to 50.5 million in 2008 due to automation, technological and organisational innovations, as well as increase in employment in services. Assuming that productivity will grow at a similar rate, as in the decade prior to the crisis, that is, 2.7% per year and that demand levels will not shift dramatically, employment in manufacturing in developed countries will drop from 12% in 2010 to below 10% by 2030. Maintaining manufacturing at current levels would mean an end to productivity growth or a demand for end product of the production sector by 50%, which is neither practically possible, nor desirable (*Manyka J. et al., 2013: 26*)[58].

The tendency described above is currently similar in Latvia. According to the population census of 2011, the highest number of employers was in the sector of services – 25% of the total employment in the country. The trade and commercial services sector made up 20% each and the manufacturing industry constituted 13% (Report on the Economic Development of Latvia, 2012: 78)[59]. As it can be concluded from the report of the Latvian Ministry of Economy, the most rapid growth of employment in 2013 in comparison with 2012 is expected in the processing industry (by 62 000 or 5.1%) and in several services

---

[57]Manyka J et al.Manufacturing the future: the next era of global growth and Innovation, McKinsey Global Insitute, McKinsey Operations Practise, November 2012, p.3. [Retrieved: 21.03.2013.]. Available at: http://www.mckinsey.com/insights/manufacturing/the_future_of_manufacturing

[58]Manyka J et al.Manufacturing the future: the next era of global growth and Innovation, McKinsey Global Institute, McKinsey Operations Practise, November 2012. p. 26. [Retrieved: 21.03.2013.]. Available at: http://www.mckinsey.com/insights/manufacturing/the_future_of_manufacturing

[59]Report On the Economic Development of Latvia.[Retrieved: 31.03.2013.]. Available at: http://www.em.gov.lv/images/modules/items/tsdep/zin_2012_2/2012_dec.pdf

sectors – the ICT sector (by 3 400 or 15.1%) professional and technical services (by 2 700 or 3.9%) as well as finance and real estate sectors (by 4 200 or .5% in total). A significant growth is also expected in construction (Report on the Economic Development of Latvia, 2012: 82)[60].

At present the role of services sector in the development of manufacturing companies plays a more and more pivotal role, e.g., design, logistics, advertising, training etc. Between 2000 and 2011 the export of services in the advanced economies has grown faster than the export of goods (Report on the Economic Development of Latvia, 2012: 15)[61]. Manufacturers are more active in using various services offered by companies in this sector. Nevertheless, just like manufacturing companies are increasing demand for such services as IT, logistics, transport, trade etc., the services are also increasing demand for produced goods. For example, in the USA for every 'input' dollar producers use services for 0.19 cents, thus creating a 900 milliard USD demand for services, while the services sector creates a 1.4 trillion USD for manufactured goods a year (*Manyka J et al. , 2013: 3*)[62].

The described trend can also be observed in the case of the video game "Angry Birds". The Finnish game became very popular quickly and the "Angry Birds" on the market were also offered in the form of toys, coffee mugs, bed linen etc. on the market. The future challenges will depend on fluctuations in demand (a more rapid increase in developing countries) and also opportunities for quick innovations based on new technologies and methods. As a result of advances in IT, a new "Forms of Intelligence" can be created and, for example, Ericsson is developing a project "Connected Devices" whose aim is to connect 50 billion things in one operating network (*Ericsson,* 2013)[63].

---

[60]Op. cit., p 82.

[61]Op. cit., p 15.

[62]Manyka J et al.Manufacturing the future: the next era of global growth and Innovation, McKinsey Global Insitute, McKinsey Operations Practise. [Retrieved: 21.03.2013.]. Available at:
http://www.mckinsey.com/insights/manufacturing/the_future_of_manufacturing

[63]http://www.ericsson.com/thinkingahead/technology_insights

In the meantime, new technologies increase the role of information, create a demand for services of the software industry that is facing a rapid growth, promoting the efficiency of business companies and public organisations and diversity in the supplies.

APPROACHES TO AND METHODOLOGY OF INNOVATION IN COMPANIES

Recently a vast number of scientific papers and academic journals have published articles on topics related to the necessity of innovations, as it is widely admitted that without innovations companies quickly lose their competiveness.

Latvia has already acknowledged the need to shift from the currently dominant sectors with a low added value to much more productive and globally competitive industries. In order to ensure economic growth in the long-term, Latvia has set its main aim to increase added value and work productivity through comprehensive processes of innovations, thereby fostering entrepreneurship with a higher added value providing support for development and implementation of new products and technologies, as well as facilitating cooperation between research and business sectors (Innovation portal, 2013)[64].

The key factors for innovations are as follows (*Oslo Manual, 2005: 46)[65]*:

1. Enhancement of companies' operating results;
2. Enhancement of productivity (for instance, as a result of organisational processes and innovations), resulting in reduced costs, in this way giving a chance to gain more profit from the existing market prices. Or by setting lower prices and a higher markup;
3. An enhanced potential for innovations;
4. Increased ability for competiveness or provision for a competitive advantage.

---

[64] Inovāciju portāls. Available at : http://www.innovativelatvia.lv/inovacijas-abc/inovacijas-politika-latvija

[65] OECD, Eurostat.*Oslo Manual: Guidelines for Collecting and Interpreting Innovation Data,* 3rd ed.Farnham: Ashgate Publishing Group, 2005. 46 p. ISBN: 978-9-2640-1310-0 .

The currently available academic and scientific literature on the topic of innovations is so diverse and extensive that indeed it becomes difficult to follow some specific issues in this field. Researchers that analyse this topic from different viewpoints have offered differing definitions. It must be acknowledged that perception of innovations is modified with the pace of time and reflects changes in the environment. Despite the diversity of opinions there is a unanimous understanding of two key concepts regarding the essence of innovations, namely: innovation is a process and its effect can be controlled in order to influence the results. Thereby the management of innovations is a process of creating and embedding this value in the chain of business processes in a particular environment in which the company functions in order to raise competiveness and achieve its objectives.

Among researchers there is a common understanding that innovation is a process; as a result, a certain profit is gained for both the company and the consumer.

The Law on Official Publications and Legal Information of Latvia prescribes that "innovation is implementation of new ideas, developments and technologies of a scientific, technical, social, or cultural field or other areas in a product or service" (Law on Scientific Activity, 2013)[66]". Unfortunately, this definition emphasises only the realisation of new ideas in a product or a service, without indicating such an important field of business innovations as optimisation of a company's processes, formation of new supply channels and cooperation, development of new markets, implementation of new management methodology etc. Not only is the offer of new or improved products in the market important for the process of innovations, but also the launch of of such new activities in every company that promotes the reduction of costs and entry into new markets.

Efficient innovation management is a great challenge for business leaders as a wide range of factors influences the success or failure, including available resources, capabilities of the employees, the process of idea generation, management of the processes, potential of the environment and the requirements etc. Awareness of the best ways businesses can

---

[66] Law on Scientific Activity. [Retrieved: 05.05.2013.]. Available at: http://www.likumi.lv/doc.php?id=107337

facilitate innovative work is essential, nevertheless the most important innovation management aspects are only shaping now, as innovation management differs widely among industries, at different stages of businesses and it also depends on the size of the company.

THE ESSENCE OF NON-TECHNOLOGICAL INNOVATIONS

If in recent past the world was focusing on technological innovations, then due to changes of the operating environment as well as broader opportunities, the role of non-technological innovations is getting more and more prominent. Technological innovations are a process in whose frame new or advanced technologies are further developed and commercialised. Traditional characteristics of innovations refer to product and process innovations, linking both with new or improved technologies. Unfortunately, this approach does not give a complete picture of the diversity of innovations and was criticised as it ignored essential business activity elements, such as marketing, external relationships etc. Non-technological innovations are new organisational or marketing methods that are introduced in the company and ensure a rise in value for clients and businesses (*Schmidt T., Rammer C., n.a.*)[67]. Thereby a broader understanding of innovations is necessary, wherewith a broader range of issues needs to be looked into in a field of non-technological innovations in order to describe the diversity of innovations and gain a wider scope of understanding.

The variety of non-technological innovations is vast and it opens up opportunities not only for businesses but also in the public sector. Business management resorts to such non-technological innovations as marketing innovations, ecological innovations, business model innovations, innovations of services, innovations of interested parties, design-driven innovations, brand-driven innovations, supply chain innovations, financial innovations etc. Technologies enhance the role of collaborative and open innovations in the operation of company. Non-technological innovations can be attributed not only to the work of businesses but also to public administration. In order to facilitate the

---

[67]Schmidt T., Rammer C. Non-technological and technological innovations: strange bedfellows. Discussion paper No 07-052, p.3. Available: ftp://ftp.zew.de/pub/zew-docs/dp/dp07052.pdf

introduction and development of non-technological innovations in companies, the business managers have to acknowledge the role of these innovations in society and in the business model of the company.

The rapidly changing environment determines the need for businesses to organise the process of innovation management in order to most efficiently combine technological opportunities with non-technological innovations, which determines the development of different competences in the company e.g. marketing and management skills, organisational competences etc. Hence, combining various competences, skills and opportunities increases the capacity of the company to introduce innovations, both technological and non-technological (*Mothe C., Thi Nguyen U. T.,2010: 313*)[68].

Usually innovations are associated with completely new or upgraded technological processes or products (*Doloreux, D., et.al., 2010: 187*)[69]. This is confirmed by the fact that most research on innovations and innovation systems is based on data from companies in the field of manufacturing or organisations that support technological innovations in manufacturing, while service sector businesses are mainly regarded as consumers of innovations in these pieces of research: as passive players, who adapt technologies created in the field of manufacturing (*Doloreux, D., 2010: 3*)[70]; as a consequence research mainly explores innovations of technological kind. Technological innovations are concerned with creation or use of new technologies, e.g. new technical knowledge or new inventions etc. whereas the basis of non-technological innovations can also be new business methods, models, new organisational concepts or other intangible approaches to change the business activities, that is, they should not necessarily include changes in technologies (*Schmidt, T., Rammer, C., 2007: 4*)[71].

---

[68]Mothe C., Thi Nguyen U. T.,The link between non-technological innovations and technical innovation. European Journal of Innovation Management. Vol. 13. No. 3, 2010, p. 313. ISSN: 1460-1060

[69]Doloreux, D., Freel, M., Shearmur, R.*Konwledge-Intensive Business Services: Geography and Innovation.* Farnham: Ashgate Publishing Group, 2010. 187 p. ISBN: 978-0-7546-9758-9

[70]Doloreux, D., Freel, M., Shearmur, R.*Konwledge-Intensive Business Services: Geography and Innovation.* Farnham: Ashgate Publishing Group, 2010. 3 p. ISBN: 978-0-7546-9758-9

[71]Schmidt, T., Rammer, C.*Non-technological and technological innovation: Strange Bedfellows? ZEW – Centre for European Economic Research Discussion Paper, No. 07-052, 2007. 4 p. Available at: ftp://ftp.zew.de/pub/zew-docs/dp/dp07052.pdf*

It has been proved by research that the combination of technological and non-technological innovations in companies leave a positive impact on company performance and the ability to efficiently introduce innovations in the market. As one of the performance indicators that is positively influenced by technological and non-technological innovation combinations is turnover growth and consequently growth of productivity. At the same time it needs to be taken into consideration that this effect can be attributed only to organisational and product innovation combination. As a result of research, it has been concluded that businesses which successfully combine technological and organisational innovations, and communication skills with customers, will introduce more innovations into the market (*Mothe C., Thi Nguyen U. T., 2010: 313)*[72].

GROWING SIGNIFICANCE OF NON-TECHNOLOGICAL INNOVATIONS IN BUSINESS MANAGEMENT

Non-technological innovations are getting more important along with a growing significance of the service sector in economy, the production sector included. Non-technological innovations, for instance, marketing and organisational innovations, are often regarded as particularly important for businesses in the service sector (*Vahter P., Masso J. , 2011)*[73].

As *T. Schmidt* and *C. Rammer* point out,technological innovations can be characterised by considerable investment in the development process (including purchase of fixed and intangible assets and expenses for R&D), a high level of uncertainty that limits the opportunities to attract external capital; it is also subject of information leakage, therefore one of the ways to protect new technologies is patent. By contrast, implementation costs

---

[72]Mothe C., Thi Nguyen U. T.,*The link between non-technological innovations and technical innovation. European Journal of Innovation Management. Vol. 13. No. 3, 2010, p. 313. ISSN: 1460-1060*

[73]Vahter P., Masso J. The Link between Innovation and Productivity in Estonia's Service Sectors. Michigan: The William Davidson Institute, 2011 [Retrieved: 22.01.2012]. Available at: *http://ssrn.com/abstract=1788918*

for non-technological innovations can be considerably lower than those of non-technological innovations (*Schmidt, T., Rammer, C. , 2007: 4*).

In comparison with technological innovations, non-technological innovations have a lower level of uncertainty, because these innovations are based on a business method or marketing techniques that have already been developed, thus decreasing the risk of failure. For example, organisational innovations mostly are company specific and are difficult to imitate. Marketing innovations could be an exception, as they are subject to information leakage more often though they can create a short-term effect. New business organisation methods can decrease costs per unit and show the same result regarding profit as process innovations. As organisational innovations are difficult to copy, the implementer can gain an advantage over competitors (*Schmidt, T., Rammer, C., 2007: 6)*[74].

Non-technological innovations include new business methods, models, new organisational concepts, changes in organisational structure, new marketing methods, as well as other non-technological approaches to reach the business objectives. The proof of the growing significance of non-technological innovations is the latest document issued by the Organisation for Economic Co-operation and Development (OECD), the revised 3rd edition of 2005: *Oslo Manual Guidelines for Collecting and Interpreting Innovation Data*. This paper has not lost its topicality and urges to look at innovations in a broader context and for the first time also includes two new types of innovations in the concept: organisational and marketing innovations. In the previous OECD guideline editions the focus was on product and process innovations, including the organisational innovations only in the Appendix without addressing marketing innovations at all (*Oslo Manual, 2005: 3*) [75].

---

[74]Schmidt, T., Rammer, C.*Non-technological and technological innovation: Strange Bedfellows?* ZEW – Centre for European Economic Research Discussion Paper, No. 07-052, 2007. 6 p. Available at: *ftp://ftp.zew.de/pub/zew-docs/dp/dp07052.pdf*
[75]OECD, Eurostat. *Oslo Manual: Guidelines for Collecting and Interpreting Innovation Data,* 3rd ed.Farnham: Ashgate Publishing Group, 2005. 3 p. ISBN: 978-9-2640-1310-0

Usually innovations are associated with completely new or improved technological processes or products (*Doloreux, D., et.al., 2010: 187*)[76]. This is confirmed by the fact that most pieces of research on innovations and innovation systems are based on data from companies in the field of manufacturing or organisations that support technological innovations in manufacturing, while service sector businesses are mainly regarded as consumers of innovations I this research: as passive players, who adopt technologies created in the field of manufacturing (*Doloreux, D., 2010: 3*)[77]; that is why in research mainly explores technological. Nevertheless over last decades we observe changes in the proportion of production and service sectors in the economy of developed countries, as the service sector becomes more prominent in terms of employment and added value.

Issues about non-technological innovations were included in the Community Innovation Statistics 2004, to be more precise in the survey of the 3rd edition of the Oslo Manual whose results form the basis for data of the Community Innovation Statistics that is also the main source of information on analysis of innovations in Europe (*Community Innovation Statistics, 2010*)[78]. The call of European Council emphasises the need to view the term "innovations" in a broader way, encouraging to include technological and non-technological innovations as well as innovations of the business model, ecological innovations, public sector innovations, open innovations, social innovations and others (*Conclusions on Innovation Union for Europe*, 2010) [79].

Innovations and their development form the key questions included in the European growth strategy for 2020, as due to the persistent tendencies of society aging and growing pressure of globalisation, the future development of European economies and new jobs

---

[76]Doloreux, D., Freel, M., Shearmur, R.*Konwledge-Intensive Business Services: Geography and Innovation*. Farnham: Ashgate Publishing Group, 2010. 187 p. ISBN: 978-0-7546-9758-9

[77]Doloreux, D., Freel, M., Shearmur, R.*Konwledge-Intensive Business Services: Geography and Innovation*. Farnham: Ashgate Publishing Group, 2010. 3 p. ISBN: 978-0-7546-9758-9

[78] Community Innovation Statistics (CIS).Brussels, European Commision. [Retrieved: 22.01.2012]. Available at: *http://epp.eurostat.ec.europa.eu/portal/page/portal/microdata/cis*

[79] Council of the European Union. *Conclusions on Innovation Union for Europe: 3049th COMPETITIVENESS (Internal Market, Industry, Research and Space) Council meeting*. . Brussels: Council of the European Union [Retrieved: 3.06.2012] Available at: http://www.consilium.europa.eu/uedocs/cms_data/docs/pressdata/en/intm/118028.pdf

will depend on the product and services sector innovations, as well as such non-technological innovations as business models *(Innovation Union, 2010)*[80].

Non-technological innovations, such as, for example, marketing and organisational innovations, are often regarded as being exceptionally important in service sector businesses; with the growing role of the service sector, the non-technological innovations are playing a more vital role *(Vahter P., Masso J., 2011)*[81]. The role of non-technological innovations is emphasised for the service sector; they are also pivotal for manufacturers in order to increase operational effectiveness and product promotion. Nowadays non-technological innovations are as important as traditional technological innovations in both the manufacturing and service sector businesses *(Jeannerat H., Crevoisier O., 2011: 31)*[82].

Marketing innovations involve introduction of new products in the market that entails important changes in the project, packaging, placement, promotion or price formation of the product *(Jeannerat H., Crevoisier O., 2011: 49)*[83]. These innovations are typically focused on markets and consumers and by nature they have a vital role in the whole process of innovation and the company's performance in general[84]. In connection with organisational innovations, the focus is on organisational structures, ability to adopt to the environment and technological changes, and the processes connected with the rise of personnel competences.

---

[80] Innovation Union, turning ideas into jobs, green growth and social progress. Brussels, European Commision. [Retrieved: 22.01.2012]. Available at: Available at: *http://ec.europa.eu/research/innovation-union/index_en.cfm*
[81] Vahter P., Masso J. The Link between Innovation and Productivity in Estonia's Service Sectors. [*tiešsaiste*]. Michigan: The William Davidson Institute, 2011 [skatīts 22.01.2012]. Pieejams*http://ssrn.com/abstract=1788918*
[82] Jeannerat H., Crevoisier O., Non-technological innovation and multi-local territorial knwoledge Dynamics in the Swiss watch industry. International Journal of Innovation and Regional Development. Vol. 3. No. 1, 2011, p. 31.
° Op. cit., p 49.
[84] *Oslo Manual: Guidelines for Collecting and Interpreting Innovation Data,* 3rd ed.OECD, Eurostat.. Farnham: Ashgate Publishing Group, 2005. 14 p. ISBN: 978-9-2640-1310-0

One of organisational innovations is the so-called lean management that initially was developed in manufacturing processes *(Niederkorn M., Ruffini C., 2008)*[85]. The Lean management method can be applied by different services sector companies, e.g., enhancement of processes in credit institutions. The implementation of lean management is related to such advantages as faster activities, lower costs, higher quality products and improved client experience *(Garrigues F., Tan M. , 2008)*[86].

As a result of introduction of new organisational methods several improvements can be carried out in a company *(Garrigues F., Tan M., 2008)* [87]:

- enhancement of quality of performance (increasing demand) and efficiency (reducing costs);
- enhanced ability to create and gain new knowledge that can serve as a basis for innovations;
- creation of new skills.

Regardless of the essence of the term 'ecological innovations', it is used in various contexts that can decrease its practical value. Ecological innovations usually refer to new technologies that improve both economy and environment indicators while the explanations of this term also include organisational and social changes, in order to promote competiveness and sustainable development of a company. Ecological innovations have become a crucial issue due to fundamental climate changes; they have increased the topicality of this issue on the global agenda.

An ecological innovation is any kind of innovation in an enterprise that evokes and enhances important and visible success factors for sustainable development, reducing the

---

[85]Niederkorn M., Ruffini C. *Banking on lean for a competitive edge.*[*tiešsaiste*]. McKinsey&Company, 2008 [skatīts 2012. gada 21. maijā]. Available at:
http://www.mckinsey.com/App_Media/Reports/Financial_Services/Banking_On_Lean_For_A_Competitive_Edge.pdf
[86]Garrigues F., Tan M. Adapting lean for customized bank processes.[*tiešsaiste*]. McKinsey&Company, 2008 [skatīts 2012. gada 3. jūnijā]. Available at:
https://www.mckinseyquarterly.com/Adapting_lean_for_customized_bank_processes_2181
[87]Ibid.

impact left on nature, improving ability to resist against pressures on the environment or succeeding in more responsible and efficient use of natural resources. The main factors influencing ecological innovations are global competition, scarcity of natural resources and climate changes that have created a situation that makes businesses worldwide introduce ecological innovations. With the help of ecological innovations companies can increase their competiveness; the global trend of fighting against environmental problems and living in an environmentally-friendly way has been set and hence businesses are more likely to attract costumers with 'green' products, processes and a general green image.

With the help of environmentally friendly or eco-friendly technologies it is possible to open up new potential markets, foster innovations, increase competiveness and create new jobs for highly qualified labour force. Ecological innovations mean benefits not only in the field of the environment. The market of ecological products and services is growing rapidly. Europe can set an example how to use the power of innovations when facing the current environmental problems, and it has the potential to increase investment in this relatively new field *(Environment. Environment fact sheets, 2010).*[88]

There is a great amount of other types of non-technological innovations, e.g., strategic innovations, business model innovations, brand promotion innovations, design promotion innovations, logistics innovations, financial management innovations and others, whose significance depends on the objectives of the company, as well as the industry, its scale of activity, and other factors.

CONNECTION BETWEEN VARIOUS TYPES OF INNOVATIONS

It has been confirmed by research that there is a connection between different types of innovations in a company, e.g., between technological and non-technological innovations *(Schmidt un Rammer, 2007: 50)* [89]. The link between organisation and process innovations

---

[88]Environment. Environment fact sheets.European Commission. [Retrieved: 15.01.2012.]. Available at: *http://ec.europa.eu/environment/pubs/pdf/factsheets/eco_innovation.pdf*
[89]Schmidt, T., Rammer, C.*Non-technological and technological innovation: Strange Bedfellows?* ZEW – Centre for European Economic Research Discussion Paper, No. 07-052, 2007. 50 p. Available at: *ftp://ftp.zew.de/pub/zew-docs/dp/dp07052.pdf*

could serve as an example. The introduction of new technologies in production or distribution can create a need for new approaches to labour organisation, and new organisational models.

The combination of technological and non-technological innovations has a positive impact on the company's performance and the ability to effectively introduce innovations. As one of performance indicators, it creates positive results in turnover, however, it needs to be taken into account that the effect can just as well be attributed to the combination of organisational and product innovations. As a result of this research it was concluded that businesses that successfully combine technological with organisational innovations and communication skills when dealing with customers, will bring more innovations to the market (*Mothe C., Thi Nguyen U. T., 2010: 313)*[90].

The impact of marketing innovations can be analysed in regard to interaction with other types of innovations *(Oslo Manual, 2005)*[91]. Product (services) innovations will bring benefits for the company only if the target groups will be introduced to them to use the new marketing methods among other approaches. Businesses have to organise the innovation process in a way to efficiently combine technological opportunities and marketing and management skills as well as organisational competences (*Mothe C., Thi Nguyen U. T., 2010: 313)*[92]. Nowadays technological knowledge is only one type of knowledge that is used in the process of manufacturing and creation of new products *(Jeannerat H., Crevoisier O., 2011: 31)*[93]. The development of new products is connected with completely new technologies and moreover they entail the necessity for new competences, structures, partners as well as processes (*Gemunden HG., 2011: 28)*[94].

Often it has been emphasised that analytical, and civil engineering knowledge, as well as knowledge about design, promotion, branding successfully complement each other in

[90]Mothe C., Thi Nguyen U. T.,*The link between non-technological innovations and technical innovation. European Journal of Innovation Management. Vol. 13. No. 3, 2010, p. 313. ISSN: 1460-1060*
[91]*Oslo Manual: Guidelines for Collecting and Interpreting Innovation Data,* 3rd ed.OECD, Eurostat, Farnham: Ashgate Publishing Group, 2005. 14 p. ISBN: 978-9-2640-1310-0
[92]Mothe C., Thi Nguyen U. T., The link between non-technological innovations and technical innovation. European Journal of Innovation Management. Vol. 13. No. 3, 2010, p. 313. ISSN: 1460-1060
[93]Jeannerat H., Crevoisier O., Non-technological innovation and multi-local territorial knwoledge Dynamics in the Swiss watch industry. International Journal of Innovation and Regional Development. Vol. 3. No. 1, 2011, p. 31
[94]Gemunden HG., Salomo S. Schultz C, The Mixed Blessings of Technological Innovativeness for the Commercial Success of New Products. The Journal of Product Innovation Management. Vol. 28. No. 6, 2011, p. 28

industrial processes *(Jeannerat H., Crevoisier O., 2011: 31)*. By combining different competences, skills, knowledge and opportunities in this way the company capacity to introduce different innovations can be increased, both technological and non-technological innovations.

TYPES AND STRATEGIES OF INNOVATIONS

The shift to innovation economy is also determined by the ability of the business managers to ensure the use of the most up-to-date methodology in the management of the company. Taking into account the fact that the companies are not homogeneous as to their strategies, types of innovations also differ, and they can be subdivided into the following groups *(Fagerberg J. et al. , 2005: 95)*[95]:

1. Research-based manufacturers (sectors, such as electronics, bioethanol, chemical industry, pharmaceuticals etc.)
2. Information-intense services (sectors of finance, retail trade, publishing, travel industry, telecommunications, logistics etc.)
3. Suppliers-dominant businesses (agriculture, traditional manufacturers etc.)
4. Large-scale enterprises (suppliers of raw materials, producers of commodities etc.)
5. Specialised-supplier companies (car industry, producers of appliances, software, advertising, design, architecture developers etc)

In all the previously mentioned businesses next to the technological solutions such non-technological innovations can be used in order to ensure efficient innovation management process: marketing, value, business model, ecological, organisational, branding, design-driven innovations etc. Businesses, that successfully combine technological, organisational innovations and communication skills when dealing with customers, will introduce more innovations in the market *(Mothe C., Thi Nguyen U. T., 2010: 313)*[96].

Technological solutions that ensure innovations in research-based companies stem from scientific discoveries (inventions) and depend on the knowledge and skills of employees in the company. The main tasks of innovation strategies are by using the latest accessible scientific discoveries and technologies to create new knowledge, enabling new discoveries,

---

[95] Fagerberg J. et al. The Oxford Handbook of Innovation, OxfordUniversity Press, 2005, p. 95.
[96] Mothe C., Thi Nguyen U. T.,*The link between non-technological innovations and technical innovation. European Journal of Innovation Management. Vol. 13. No. 3, 2010, p. 313. ISSN: 1460-1060*

commercialising with the help of which it is possible to better address the changing needs of society.

Without investment in R&D a large proportion of innovative activities depend solely on highly qualified employees, and knowledge focused organisational structure, as well as cooperation with other companies and research institutions (*Oslo Manual, 2005*)[97].

In information-intense companies the most important task is to create and facilitate efficient functioning of complex IT systems, in order to process information, especially in the dissemination systems and to adapt the service for the changing needs of consumers. In such companies the key aims of innovation strategies are the creation of new products and processes, development and management of complex IT systems, coordination of IT opportunities and user needs.

Research provides evidence that a difference between businesses from different sectors becomes more obvious here. For instance, telecommunication and finance sector companies tend to focus more on product innovations. That in turn is explained by the fact that in the field of telecommunications, a big role is played by technological development, and in particular the development of mobile phones. While transport and trade companies focus more on services rather than product innovations. This can be due to the fact that usually the demand in the transport and trade sectors is somewhat equal for all companies *(Oke A., 2007: 564-587)*[98].

In supplier-dominant businesses the main technological solutions come from production input-resource suppliers, management of manufacturing technologies and the consumers. The key aims of innovation strategies are based on non-technological solutions, use of IT in finance management and distribution of the product, in order to be flexible towards the needs of the consumers. It is essential to use the latest technologies that are available in the market to increase the competiveness of the company and use the advantages created by IT for the introduction of new systems in distribution, logistics, transactions, in order to operatively adapt to the needs of consumers. Commercial banks,

[97]*Oslo Manual: Guidelines for Collecting and Interpreting Innovation Data,* 3rd ed. OECD, Eurostat. Farnham: Ashgate Publishing Group, 2005. 46 p. ISBN: 978-9-2640-1310-0

[98] Oke A. Innovation types and innovation management practices in service companies. International Journal of Operations & Product Management, Vol. 26, Iss. 6, pp. 564-587, 2007

for instance, use IT solutions that are bought from the leading IT companies as an outsourcing service.

In large-scale enterprises the sources of new technologies is production of the product, effect of learning, supplier and designer services, maintenance of complex manufacturing systems, provision of logistics etc. The key aims of innovation strategy are to ensure a cost efficient and safe manufacturing process and integration of the best practices. The latest computer technologies (especially simulation and modelling) offer a broad range of opportunities how to save time, and financial resources to develop and test the product prototypes. The Food Union, for instance, constantly invests in high-tech manufacturing process and innovative product marketing, so that dairy products produced in Latvia would become a global quality standard and be competitive in Europe and also worldwide. About 25 million was invested to set up plants in 2011 and 2012, out of which more than 11 million was invested in modern technologies to produce ice-cream. Such features as 3D technologies are used in the process of production; liquid nitrogen is used to produce frosting etc. The Food Union ensures maintenance of a full cycle of milk-processing using only fresh milk. Goods are produced in a closed milk-processing cycle, which includes milkseparation, mechanicalhomogenisationandthermal treatment. This is followed by further processing as part of the automated or the closed system, depending on the product type. At the end of the processing cycle, milk, kefir, cheese, yogurt, ice-cream and other Food Union products are ready for pre-packaging and are stored in the Food Union warehouse (Food Union, 2013)[99]. The above example shows that the company uses both technological and non-technological innovations, for instance, marketing innovations, brand-driven innovations and others.

In specialised supplier companies, the main sources of technologies are design and the demand of early users. The strategy of innovations is focused on response to user needs, hence adaption of technologies to the needs of users and a strong relationship with the leading users. For example, the Latvian company *"Biograph Organic Sweets"* has invested 60 000 LVL in Jelgava and it has created an ecological facility to produce berries and fruit, as the Chairman of the Board Didzis Desainis has announced to the news agency BNS. He has informed them that *"Biograph Organic Sweets"* has acquired the support of the JIC Business Incubator and a loan from "Latvijas Hipotēku un zemes banka" (Latvian Mortgage Bank) as part of their start-up programme. For the purchase of manufacturing

---

[99] Food Union homepage. [Retrieved: 05.05.2013.] Available at: http://www.foodunion.lv/lv/razojam/latvia.

equipment, co-financing from the Rural Support ServiceProgramme has been attracted as part of the programme "purchase of additional manufacturing equipment for the production of agricultural goods with a high added value to ensure ongoing operation and to increase production capacity". Desainis has noted that *"Biograph Organic Sweets"* produces fruit cubes that are made from ecologically pure berries and apples, adding ecological sugar and natural fruit pectin. At present the company produces three different sorts of fruit cubes – made from raspberries, bilberries and black currants (see Figure 1), while in the future it plans to expand the assortment and produce sweets from at least 12 different home-grown vegetables, berries and fruit, including pumpkin and rowan berries. The company was founded at the end of 2010, and their paid equity capital has amounted to 2000 LVL. There are two owners with an equal share: Didzis Desainis and Renārs Nadrickis" *(Biograph Organic Sweets, 2013)*[100]. The company makes good use of ecological innovations, marketing innovations, and branding innovations that facilitate product promotion in the market.

Figure 1. Design of SIA *Biograph Organic Sweets*

[100]"Biograph organic sweets" par 60 tūkstošiem latu izveido ogu un augļu saldumu ražotni. BNS, 18.12.13. [Retrieved: 11.02.13.]Available at: http://www.mansbizness.lv/

FUTURE CONCEPTIONS OF INNOVATIONS

On the basis of research carried out together with 100 experts worldwide the following interconnected innovation concepts have been singled out:

1. Costumer-based innovations;
2. Proactive Business model innovations;
3. High speed/low risk innovations;
4. Frugal innovations;
5. Integrated innovations *(R.Eager, 2011)*[101].

Consumer based innovations. The results of the research disclose that investment in relationship to the customer is the main priority for a company; and it is promoted by wider social networks that create a comprehensive costumer experience. Due to these changes businesses need to be more flexible and creative in choosing the mode of interaction with the customer. Under the influence of social networks, competition shifts from price formation to establishment of relationships with the client and adaption to the changing environment of the market. Companies have to use complex approaches of open innovations as there is ongoing transition from "any source of innovation" to open connection of innovations with business strategies with an aim to ensure costumer loyalty.

Proactive business model innovations. The business model determines how values are developed and maintained in the chain processes of value creation, both on operational and strategic level. New tendencies in management of business models are connected with the need to focus on creation of additional value for the public and not only on desire to make a profit or adapt a business model to different market environments and new markets.

Frugal innovations. Frugal innovations foresee the formation of innovations for markets with a lower income, for it is necessary to view the emerging markets not only as a source of lower costs but also as product outlets and a source of innovations. Currently, companies in China, India and Brasil enter new markets with innovations. There is an

---

[101]R.Eager, F. van Oene, C.Boulton, D. Ross, C.Dekeyser. The future of Innovation Management: next 10 years, 2011.[Retrieved 11.02.2013.] Available at:*http://www.adlittle.com/prism-articles.html?&view=379*

ongoing revision of the essence of innovations – from 'more' to 'less'. Frugality becomes an integral part of innovative thinking. Availability also becomes a component of the innovative mindset that defines more flexible and open approaches to the needs of innovation management.

High speed or low risk innovations. High speed or low risk innovations predict the need to reduce time of entering a market, e.g., by envisaging gradual product promotion (a low number of initial product versions that are gradually developed) as well as formation of global innovation management teams. Due to the impact of new technologies, businesses can ensure trials and experiments without meaningful investments, by carrying out prototyping, 3D visualisation, at the same time expanding attraction of the costumer from the very beginning of product development.

Integrated innovations. Integrated innovations forecast integration in business strategies at all levels and functions of company activity. That entails systematic use of formal innovation tools and approaches.

How women and elderly drive innovation?

Women have valuable insights when it comes to devising products or services that better serve female clients and customers. For companies tasked with understanding female consumers, tapping women improves the likelihood their success of activities. Women's ideas won't translate into marketable products or services unless leadership backs them therefore culture of organization matters. Culture is crucial to unlocking women's insights where all voices get heard and everyone feels welcome to contribute to success of company activities. Leaders who are willing to change direction based on women's input are more likely to tap into winning ideas.

Retired people becoming dominant sociodemographic group in many countries. Only few companies recognize the potential benefits of exploiting this market segment. Elderly are not homogeneous groupthey areindividuals with own preferences and habits and user-driven approach in creating innovations takes into consideration these diferences. Therefore it is important to ensure that the elderly plays important role in project team and are involved broader in the companies activities. User - driven innovation is based on approach having access to elderly's life and to understand their point of view to build

145

relationship with elderly in order to feel them safe and be able to express what they think. Is it crucial to understand better life and learn about changing needs of elderly? Focus group meetings can be organized to get deeper insights into problems faced by elderly seeking for best solutions offered and improving quality of life of elderly.

Conclusions

When reflecting on the development of economy in the 21st century, the main focus needs to be set on innovation in the broadest sense of the word, as well as innovation ecosystems that create innovation-friendly environment, labour productivity growth and facilitation of export. If in the last century more attention was paid to technological innovations, now, in the 21st century due to a better understanding of the essence of innovations, we see constant growth of the significance and the role of non-technological innovations in entrepreneurship and economies. Therefore it is essential to understand the core meaning of innovations, their vast diversity and the ways how it affects the structure of economies, and hence also the significance of innovations. Over the last decades, the economies of developed countries witness changes in the proportion of production and service sectors; the service sector is becoming more important in connection with employment and added value. Therefore the meaning of non-technological innovations is also expanding, owing to services that become a more important part of manufacturing companies. The role of non-technological innovations also becomes crucial in service sector businesses.

At present the life cycle of a product is getting shorter, and more intense competition can be observed among companies. Customers are also changing; they have become more demanding, for the 21st century attaches importance not only to the functional aspects and the quality of the product, but also to emotions, including consumer satisfaction. The world is constantly changing, and the business leaders have to acknowledge the global challenges, continually follow the trends in new technologies, new consumer needs and the needs and the opportunities of the company in the market, offering new or updated products or technological solutions. New technologies change the boundaries of industries and new ones emerge that provide new opportunities for business development and meet the needs of the customers. Clients become product co-developers and partners, former competitors become companions; the business models are changing and hence the mindset and management approaches of business leaders also have to change. All these factors determine the need for management innovations. We need to take into consideration the fact that companies are not homogenous and innovation types and strategies applied differ. Management approaches and methods change due to a broader understanding of the essence of innovation, including both technological and non-technological innovations, and all the advantages provided. Business leaders have to acknowledge the gist of both technological and non-technological innovations and their inter-relations as well as trends in development in order to ensure efficient and meaningful innovation management in their companies, as well the role of women and elderly in fostering innovations both technological and nontechnological innovations

The increasing meaning of the service sector in Latvian economy testifies to the fact that the structure of economy has developed according to the model of advanced economies. In order to ensure economic development, policy makers have to focus not only on industrial policy, but on innovations policy that determines sustainable development of economy, without focusing on a particular sector at the cost of others and by acknowledging economy as a unified whole and the contributions of both sectors to the future development of economy. Innovation policy has to be centred on the creation of favourable ecosystems for innovations, paying particular attention to deployment of innovation potential of women and elderly thus ensuring long term competitiveness and increasing the well being of society.

List of References

1. LR Zinātniskās darbības likums. Tiešsaiste (skatīts 05.05.2013.) Pieejams: http://www.likumi.lv/doc.php?id=107337
2. Doloreux, D., Freel, M., Shearmur, R. Konwledge-Intensive Business Services: Geography and Innovation. Farnham: Ashgate Publishing Group, 2010, 246 p.
3. OECD, Eurostat.Oslo Manual: Guidelines for Collecting and Interpreting Innovation Data, 3rd ed. Farnham: Ashgate Publishing Group, 2005, 164 p.
4. Carsten Schult Alexander Kock, Hans Georg Gemünden, Søren Salomo. The Mixed Blessings of Technological Innovativeness for the Commercial Success of New Products. The Journal of Product Innovation Management. Vol. 28. No. 1, 2011, p.28 – 43.

5. Mothe C., Thi Nguyen U. T.,The link between non-technological innovations and technical innovation. European Journal of Innovation Management. Vol. 13. No. 3, 2010.

6. Jeannerat H., Crevoisier O., Non-technological innovation and multi-local territorial knwoledge Dynamics in the Swiss watch industry. International Journal of Innovation and Regional Development. Vol. 3. No. 1, 2011.

7. Oke A. Innovation types and innovation management practices in service companies. International Journal of Operations & Product Management, Vol. 26, Iss.6, 2007.

Internet sources:

1. Manyka J et al.Manufacturing the future: the next era of global growth and Innovation, McKinsey Global Institute, McKinsey Operations Practise, November 2012 . Tiešsaiste (skatīts 21.03.2013.). Pieejams: http://www.mckinsey.com/insights/manufacturing/the_future_of_manufacturing

2. Pasaulē lielākais industriālo lodīšu gultņu ražotājs SKF samazinās 2500 darbavietas. 14.01.13. Tiešsaiste. Pieejams: http://news.lv/BNS/2013/01/14/Pasaule-lielakais-industrialo-lodisu-gultnu-razotajs-SKF-samazinas-2500-darbavietas

3. "Honda" Lielbritānijas rūpnīcā atlaidīs 800 darbinieku. 11.01.13. Available at: http://news.lv/BNS/2013/01/11/Honda-Lielbritanijas-rupnica-atlaidis-800-darbinieku

4. Lai samazinātu tēriņus, "Osram" likvidēs 4700 darbavietu un slēgs ražotnes.BNS, 30.11.12. Tiešsaiste (skatīts 05.05.13.) Available at: http://www.kasjauns.lv/lv/zinas/101871/spuldzisu-kompanija-osram-likvides-4700-darbavietu-un-slegs-razotnes

5. Ceturtā daļa firmu plāno samazināt darbinieku skaitu. Available at: http://www.kasjauns.lv/lv/zinas/106694/ceturtdala-zviedrijas-firmu-plano-samazinat-darbinieku-skaitu

6. Melbārzde L. Airbaltic cirps darbinieku skaitu un samazinās biļešu cenas. Available at: http://www.db.lv/razosana/transports-logistika/airbaltic-cirps-darbinieku-skaitu-un-samazinas-bilesu-cenas-253016

7. Hāka Ž. Liepājas metalurgs atlaidīs darbiniekus un samazinās algas. Available at: http://www.db.lv/finanses/investors/papildinata-liepajas-metalurgs-atlaidis-darbiniekus-un-samazinas-algas-392410

8. http://www.ericsson.com/thinkingahead/technology_insights

9. Schmidt T., Rammer C. Non-technological and technological innovations: strange bedfellows. Discussion paper No 07-052, p.3. Available at:ftp://ftp.zew.de/pub/zew-docs/dp/dp07052.pdf

10. Vahter P., Masso J. The Link between Innovation and Productivity in Estonia's Service Sectors. Michigan: The William Davidson Institute, 2011. Available at:http://ssrn.com/abstract=1788918

11. Community Innovation Statistics (CIS)Brisele: Eiropas Komisija, 2010. Available at: http://epp.eurostat.ec.europa.eu/portal/page/portal/microdata/cis

12. Council of the European Union.Conclusions on Innovation Union for Europe: 3049th COMPETITIVENESS (Internal Market, Industry, Research and Space) Council meeting.Tiešsaiste: Brussels: Council of the European Union . Available at:http://www.consilium.europa.eu/uedocs/cms_data/docs/pressdata/en/intm/118028.pdf

13. Niederkorn M., Ruffini C. Banking on lean for a competitive edge. McKinsey&Company, 2008. Available at: http://www.mckinsey.com/App_Media/Reports/Financial_Services/Banking_On_Lean_For_A_Competitive_Edge.pdf

14. Garrigues F., Tan M. Adapting lean for customized bank processes.McKinsey&Company, 2008 Available at: https://www.mckinseyquarterly.com/Adapting_lean_for_customized_bank_processes_2181

15. European Commission. Environment. Environment fact sheets. Eiropas Savienība: Eiropas Vides Komisija, 2010. Available at: http://ec.europa.eu/environment/pubs/pdf/factsheets/eco_innovation.pdf

16. Biograph organic sweets" par 60 tūkstošiem latu izveido ogu un augļu saldumu ražotni. BNS, 18.12.13. Available at: http://www.mansbizness.lv/

17. R.Eager, F. van Oene, C.Boulton, D. Ross, C.Dekeyser. The future of Innovation Management: next 10 years, 2011.Available at: http://www.adlittle.com/prism-articles.html?&view=379

18. Innovation Union Scoreboard. Available at: http://ec.europa.eu/enterprise/policies/innovation/facts-figures-analysis/innovation-scoreboard/index_en.htm, 80 pp.

19. Platace L. Neinovatīvā Latvija. Kā veicināt Latvijas konkurētspēju. 2013. Tiešsaiste. Pieejams: http://www.lvportals.lv/print.php?id=252340

Latvia'slabour market trends and challenges for entrepreneurship education

Veronika Bikse University of Liepaja

Baiba Rivza Latvia University of Agriculture

The aim of this paper is to identify the problems in implementing entrepreneurship education in Latvia's higher schools and their solutions according to the challenges of the 21st century labour market, based on a review of special literature, forecasts of Latvia's labour market, and a survey of alumni. In the paper the qualitative and quantitative changes in the labour market and their significant effect on education are shown. It is necessary to create the circumstances for the youth to develop their entrepreneurial competences in the process of entrepreneurship education, so they are capable and willing to start their own entrepreneurship and became employers themselves. The current research is performed based on a review of scientific literature, an analysis of the Latvian labour market development trends until the year 2030, and the results of the Latvian universities' alumni survey from 2006 to 2011 (4909 respondents). The research examines weather the entrepreneurship education in higher education institutions in Latvia meets the challenges of the 21st century labour market, as well as the problems are discovered and solutions are proposed. The analysis of the research topic shows that most of the respondents have not had the opportunity to develop their entrepreneurial skills during their studies, consequently after the graduation only a few have started their business and have become employers or the self-employed.

Key words: labour market trends, the new role of entrepreneurs, entrepreneurship education, entrepreneurial competences, entrepreneurial skills, promotion of entrepreneurship.

Introduction

The rapid development of information technologies causes significant changes in public life and in the labour market. A new pattern of society emerges, and values, the situation in the labour market, and attitudes to individuals and their development and value-orientation change. The role and functions of entrepreneur, as well as the knowledge, skills, and attitudes needed in establishing and managing an enterprise change.

Higher standards are set for entrepreneurship education. Several circumstances determine the urgency for it.

First, quantitative and qualitative changes in the labour market and in the production pattern. The roles of remote working and micro-enterprises in economic growth and the employment of the population continue increasing. Under the current circumstances, the role of individuals in the economy significantly changes: they become employers to themselves and, at the same time, entrepreneurs and the self-employed. It sets much higher standards for higher education – to prepare not only knowledgeable and high-qualified professionals, but, according to the challenges of the 21st century labour market, to enable new professionals to develop their entrepreneurial competences, so that they are ready, in the future, to establish their own enterprise, become self-employed individuals, or work remotely.

Second, changes in the development of human capital lead to focusing on competentindividuals as the most important precondition of competitiveness. It envisages implementing competence-based education together with entrepreneurshipeducation, thus integrating the elements of entrepreneurship education in all study programmes (courses) focused on building entrepreneurial competences. This requires a complex approach not only to tackling organisational problems in the study/training process, placing the main focus on the formation of personality and creating opportunities for self-realisation, but also to targeted entrepreneurial education management.

Research methodology

The present research reviewed the special literature, publications, documents of the European Commission and analysed, grouped, and compared the data of the survey of alumni with the 2012 study by the *Global Entrepreneurship Monitor*.

To make a forecast of Latvia's labour market, the medium-term labour market forecasts until 2020 and long-term labour market forecasts until 2030 produced by the Ministry of Economics of the Republic of Latvia were used.

Yet, to find out whether the entrepreneurship education in Latvia's higher schools meet the challenges of the 21st century labour market and what its role is in preparing youth to start entrepreneurial activity – in acquiring knowledge and developing skills –, a survey of alumni of 2006-2011 who graduated from all Latvian universities was conducted from 29 November 2011 to 14 December 2011. The survey was electronically conducted using the Internet (WAPI).

In total, 17160 individuals were sent an invitation to participate in the survey. Of the total, 6500 alumni responded. Of the total number of questionnaires, 332 were invalid, as they did not fit the target group, and additional 1259 questionnaires were incomplete. So, 4909 questionnaires were recognised as valid. Most of the respondents were women (70.4%), while men accounted for only 29.6 percent. The respondents were quite young – 81.5% were aged 18-34. Of them, 46.3% held a bachelor's degree, while 39.7% had a master's degree, and 2% – a doctoral degree. Other participants had a first or second level professional higher education.

The percentage distribution of the respondents by university was as follows: the University of Latvia – 34.1%, Riga Technical University – 28.8%, Latvia University of Agriculture – 13.4%, Liepaja University – 11.0%, Daugavpils University – 8.3%, and Riga Stradins University – 4.3%. The majority of the respondents (89%) studied only at one university. Two universities were graduated by 10%, while 1% studied at three or four universities. Among those who studied at more than one university, most – 19 percent – were the alumni of Riga Stradins University.

Depending on the education acquired by the alumni, the percentage distribution of the respondents was as follows: social sciences, business studies, and law – 37.3%; engineering, industry, and construction – 16.6%; natural sciences, mathematics, and information technologies – 14.0%; pedagogy and educational sciences – 9.7%; humanitarian sciences and the arts – 9.5%; healthcare and social welfare – 6.2%; services – 4.7%; and agriculture – 2.0%. The survey data were processed by the *Marketing and Public Opinion Research Centre* (SKDS Ltd) in November and December 2011 within the framework of the project "Universities Investment in the Latvian Economy (UILE, 2012)".

Research findings

Quantitative forecasts of the labour market in Latvia

Changes in the national economy – in the *composition of industries, in employment,* and in the percentage distribution of economically active enterprises, including the *development of micro-enterprises* and the *creation of remote jobs* – are characterised by quantitative changes in the labour market. To identify the potential trends in Latvia's labour market, the Ministry of Economics has produced forecasts for the period until 2030. The forecasts were produced based on the economic and demographic scenarios developed and expert evaluations performed. Two development scenarios were designed: the target scenario if the global economy's growth is harmonised and stable and the weak growth scenario in case its growth becomes inhomogeneous, which is characterised by lower growth rates, including a slower recovery of the EU from the sovereign debt crisis.

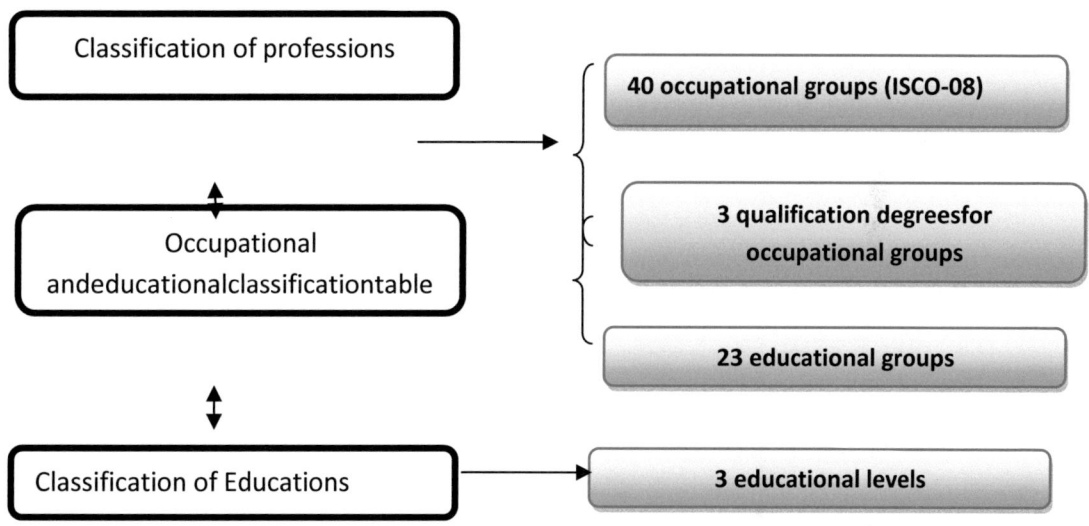

Figure 1.Aggregation of occupational and educational forecasts.

Source: Author's construction, according a forecast of Latvia's labour market (Ministry of Economics, 2012)

The Ministry of Economics labour market forecasts are based on an aggregated system of 8 economic sectors, 40 occupational groups (according to Latvia's Classification of Professions, based on ISCO-08), 23 educational fields broken down by 3 levels (according to Latvia's Classification of Educations) (Figure 1).

Latvia's labour market trends are forecasted, *first*, broken down by economic sector based on the expected changes in economic growth and labour productivity. *Second*, broken down by profession, based on the changes in the composition of professions in an economic sector.*Third*, changes in the educational levels. These changes are determined by the skills/education needed for the most demanded professions. To identify the expected changes *among economic sectors*, the target scenario assumes that Latvia's gross domestic product (GDP) might increase by 50.7% until 2020 (according to the weak growth scenario, by 34%) compared with 2011 (Table 1).

Table 1.**Changes in GDP, productivity, and employment in Latvia's economic sectors in 2020 compared with 2011 (the target scenario)**

	Number (in thousands)		Increase (%)		
Economic sectors	**Employees**	**Change**	**GDP**	**Productivity**	**Emplo yment**
Agriculture	75	-1	35.4	37.1	1.7
Manufacturing	132	17	72.3	57.2	15.1
Other industry	23	1	28.5	24.9	3.6
Construction	69	8	100.7	87.8	12.9
Commerce	172	11	48.2	41.5	6.7
Transportation and communication	79	6	51.7	43.2	8.5
Services	166	13	43.4	34.6	8.8
Public services	208	9	29.4	25.1	4.3
In total	**925**	**64**	**50.7**	**43.3**	**7.4**

Source: Author's table, according a forecast of Latvia's labour market (Ministry of Economics, 2012)

As Table 1 shows, higher growth rates than on average in the national economy may be expected in three industries: construction (100.7%), manufacturing (72.3%), and transportation (51.7%). Mainly increases in labour productivity will contribute to growth in these sectors. Along with economic growth, changes in the *composition of employment* will take place. According to the forecasts of GDP and labour productivity increases in these sectors, the greatest demand for employees in the labour market is also forecasted for these sectors. In 2020, it will exceed the level of 2011 by 15.1% in manufacturing, 12.9% in construction, and 8.5% in transportation.

In 2023, compared with 2011, the number of employees in Latvia will increase by 104 thousand. Their number will increase in all sectors, except agriculture and forestry. A relatively great increase in the number of employees will be observed in industries of services. It will exceed the level of 2011 by 15% and account for on average a fifth of the total number of employees in the economy. The growth of other economic sectors and the increasing demand for outsourcing and remote jobs will mainly contribute to growth in the industries of services.

According to the target scenario, the expected restructuring of the national economy will cause changes in the *labour market demand among the groups of professions.* The demand for high- and medium-qualified professionals will increase at a faster rate (by 92.8 thousand and 33.6 thousand, respectively, in 2030 compared with 2011). The increase will mainly take place in manufacturing and services. Yet, the demand for medium-qualified agricultural employees will sharply decrease (by 10.2 thousand until 2030). In all the sectors, the demand for low-qualified employees will decline.

The forecasts of Latvia's labour market demand broken down by *educational groups* indicate that a greater demand is forecasted for high-qualified specialists with higher education in the group *social sciences, business studies, and law.* Yet, the greatest demand for employees with secondary professional education will be observed in the group *engineering, industry, and construction* (Table 2).

Table 2.**Forecasts of Latvia's labour market demand broken down by educational levels and groups (in thousands, the target scenario)**

Educational field	Higher education		Professional secondary education	
	2020	2030	2020	2030
Education	38.0	34.9	2.7	1.8
Humanitarian sciences and arts	23.0	26.2	7.2	6.7
Social sciences, business studies, and law	137.4	156.5	33.7	32.5
Natural sciences, mathematics, and information technologies	23.9	33.5	6.6	6.5
Engineering, industry, and construction	55.3	66.4	172.4	175.3
Agriculture	9.0	9.6	17.2	14.5
Health care and social welfare	33.8	45.2	11.5	9.2
Services	15.3	19.7	40.9	46.6
Total	**336.2**	**392.7**	**292.2**	**293.1**

Source.: Author's table, according a forecast of Latvia's labour market (Ministry of Economics, 2012)

With the current composition of educations remaining the same, it is forecasted that the demand will increase only for high-qualified specialists. Such specialists will account for almost half of the entire demand in the labour market in 2030, whereas in the other educational levels the demand will decline, especially for employees with elementary and lower education, and their proportion might comprise slightly more than 10 percent. Besides, a lack of employees with both higher and secondary professional education could be observed in some educational groups (because of insufficient demand): natural sciences, engineering, industry, construction, and agriculture, whereas a lack of employees with secondary professional education will be observed in the group of social sciences, business studies, and law.

To meet the increasing demand in the labour market, the number of residents in Latvia should increase as well. The forecasts indicate that the population will decrease by almost 200 thousand over the next 30 years (to 1.8 million people). The main reason for it will be the ageing of population resulting in a greater gap between the birth and mortality rates. The number of working-age residents will decrease faster than the total population. It will result in a significant decrease in the supply of employees in the labour market. For this reason, a considerable lack of employees and a large imbalance in the labour market will emerge. Besides, if the current composition of educations remains, the demand and supply imbalance in the labour market will increase even more.

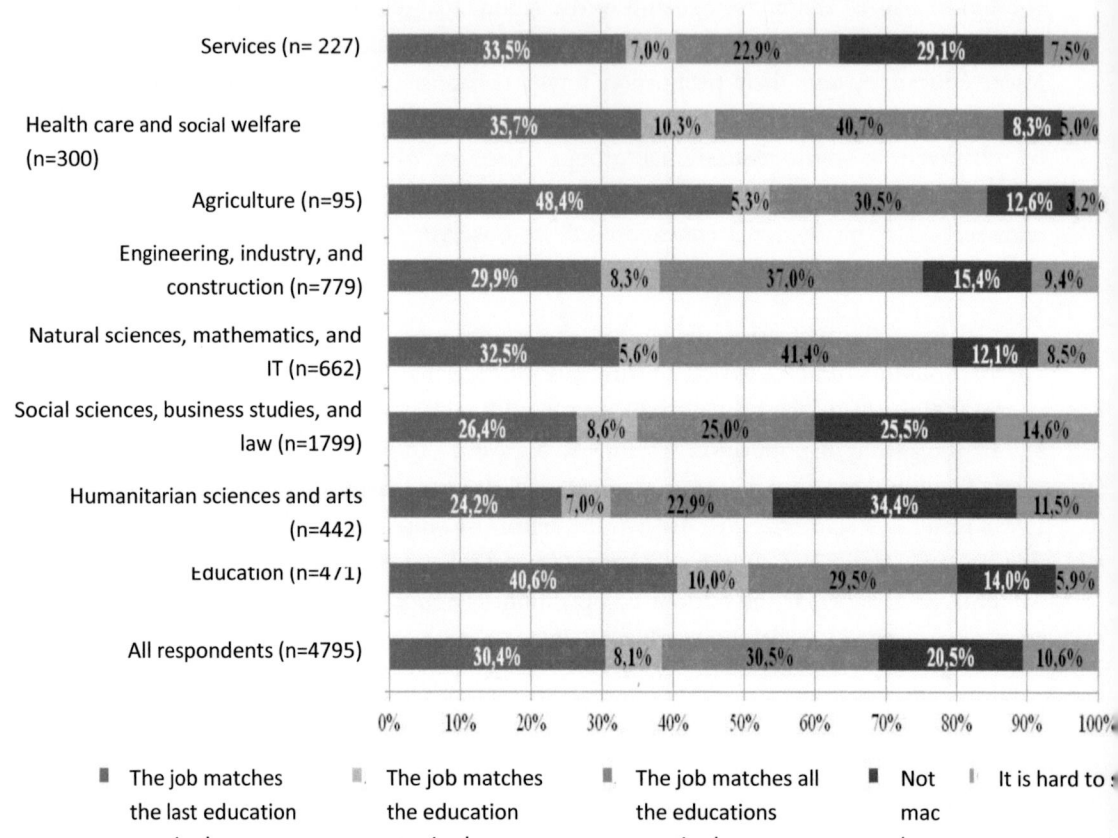

Services (n= 227): 33,5% | 7,0% | 22,9% | 29,1% | 7,5%

Health care and social welfare (n=300): 35,7% | 10,3% | 40,7% | 8,3% | 5,0%

Agriculture (n=95): 48,4% | 5,3% | 30,5% | 12,6% | 3,2%

Engineering, industry, and construction (n=779): 29,9% | 8,3% | 37,0% | 15,4% | 9,4%

Natural sciences, mathematics, and IT (n=662): 32,5% | 5,6% | 41,4% | 12,1% | 8,5%

Social sciences, business studies, and law (n=1799): 26,4% | 8,6% | 25,0% | 25,5% | 14,6%

Humanitarian sciences and arts (n=442): 24,2% | 7,0% | 22,9% | 34,4% | 11,5%

Education (n=471): 40,6% | 10,0% | 29,5% | 14,0% | 5,9%

All respondents (n=4795): 30,4% | 8,1% | 30,5% | 20,5% | 10,6%

Legend:
- The job matches the last education acquired
- The job matches the education acquired
- The job matches all the educations acquired
- Not mac
- It is hard to s

When producing labour market forecasts, it is also important to consider the changes in the *percentage distribution of economically active enterprises*. Presently, the economies of Latvia and other EU Member States are based on small and medium enterprises (SME). In 2010 in Latvia, SMEs accounted for 99.7% of the total number of economically active market sector enterprises (99.8% in the EU). In the percentage distribution of SMEs, the highest proportion in Latvia and the EU Member States belongs to micro-enterprises (91.2%). Besides, as information technologies develop, kinds of job that do not require permanent presence at an enterprise increasingly emerge; these jobs are remote from the direct production process and can be performed even at home.

Based on the quantitative analysis of Latvia's labour market, one has to conclude that in the period until 2030, compared with 2011, the demand for professionals with higher and secondary professional education will considerably increase. The roles of outsourcing and remote working as well as micro-enterprises in economic growth and employment will increase. Under such circumstances, the education system has to meet not only the quantitative economic needs but, what is more important, it has to adapt to the qualitative labour market changes to prepare competitive professionals.

Qualitative changes in the labour market and the increasing role of entrepreneurs as the self-employed

Qualitative just like quantitative changes in the labour market are mainly determined by progress in information technologies, which, along with the changes in the percentage distribution of economic sectors, enterprises, and occupations, significantly modifies the role of individuals in the production process, adding a new content to the following concepts: *entrepreneur (the self-employed), entrepreneurial ability, and entrepreneurial education,* thus assigning a much wider sense to these concepts in the context of developing *entrepreneurial competences.* It makes us seek answers to the questions on how to explain these concepts from the theoretical aspect, what competences and personal traits have to be developed to start up entrepreneurship and prepare new professionals according to the challenges of the labour market.

The initial idea of the concept *entrepreneur* refers to his/her courage and ability to risk, as "An entrepreneur acts under economically unsafe, unpredictable, and unforeseen market conditions and therefore he/she often has to take risk" (Cantillon, 1755). Later on, other economists (Say, 1855) associated the role of entrepreneur with the combination of production factors and the entrepreneur's profit. Yet, at the end of the 19th century, as soon as new trends emerged in production and large enterprises and stock companies were founded, the roles of manager and production management increased. A need arose to separate certain functions and entrust their execution to a special (specialised) category of entrepreneurs (businessmen), stating that an entrepreneur has to inherit the traits of manager or to possess a natural talent of manager (Marshall,1953*)*. Alfred Marshall was the one who for the first time in history described in detail the individual's traits and business ability that are needed to the entrepreneur to successfully manage various forms of entrepreneurship. He wrote that entrepreneurs "adventure or undertake its risks; they bring together the capital and the labour required for the work; they arrange or engineer its general plan, and superintend its minor details" (Marshall,1953).

It has to be noted that A.Marshall talks mainly about production management problems, diverse functions that have to be performed by a manager or businessman, and necessary abilities to manage an enterprise. The economist wrote that the manufacturer who makes goods not to meet special orders but for the general market, must, in his first role as merchant and organizer of production, have a thorough knowledge of things in his own trade. He must have the power of forecasting the broad movements of production and consumption, of seeing where there is an opportunity for supplying a new commodity that will meet a real want or improving the plan of producing an old commodity. He must be able to judge cautiously and undertake risks boldly; and he must of course understand the materials and machinery used in his trade (Marshall,1953).

In his works, Schumpeter conducted in-depth analyses of the role of entrepreneur in production and expanded the concept of entrepreneurial ability, stressing that an entrepreneur has to be a creative personality and an initiator of innovation. In this regard, J. Schumpeter wrote that entrepreneurial ability is the individual's ability to create innovations. An individual who can do it may be called an entrepreneur, and an innovation process may be called entrepreneurship (Schumpeter, 1983).

In the 1960's, an increasing focus had been placed on researching return on investment in relation not only to physical capital but mainly to human capital, its effects on employment, labour productivity, economic growth, and a country's competitiveness. The term human capital was introduced and a theory on human capital was developed, as well as the role of education system in building human capital was emphasised. An increasing attention was paid to the entrepreneur and to developing his/her abilities. In economics textbooks, too, several authors, for instance, McCoonnell, Brue, Lipsney, and others, along with the known economic resources – land, capital, and human labour – start using the fourth one – entrepreneurial ability or entrepreneur (McCoonnell,& Brue, 1999).

Since the *economic approach* to human capital dominated until the end of the 20th century, the functions and abilities of entrepreneur were mainly associated with meeting labour market demands. It was mainly limited to developing the personal traits needed to a manager and to acquiring knowledge and skills: to take risk to manage and effectively combine the remaining factors of production; to manage the factors to produce goods and services and introduce innovations in production in order to make profit. So, *the role of entrepreneur was to perform economic functions to ensure the successful operation of an enterprise and meet the market demand. As the most essential role of entrepreneur, the role of manager was emphasised.*

Yet, by the end of the 20th century, the demand for various services significantly rose, the proportion of micro-enterprises in the number of small and medium enterprises increased, and the role of individual in production changed. In large enterprises, too, affected by the development of information technologies, even if production expands, the number of jobs does not increase but decrease. The demand for outsourced services that are rendered remotely from an enterprise and that can be rendered even from home, in its turn, increases. For this reason, a new employment pattern emerges: individuals themselves have to establish their own enterprise, manage it, and do entrepreneurial activity. In this way, they become employers, *entrepreneurs, and the self-employed.* It evidences that nowadays the role of entrepreneur in the economy significantly changes. The same individual becomes an owner and a manager of an enterprise and a direct performer of a job, besides, in several fields. So, scientists explain the concept *entrepreneur* by the entrepreneur's ability to establish a new enterprise. "A successful entrepreneur is a manager and something more" (Misra, &Kumars,2000).

A modern entrepreneur as a shaper of his/her enterprise has to be a "self manager", i.e. to be ready to work independently, to be a generator of ideas, to plan his/her working time, to make optimal decisions, to organise his/her work, to continuously acquire new knowledge, and to tackle other problems related to entrepreneurship; the entrepreneur has to be a high-qualified specialist in a certain field. A modern entrepreneur has to be much more universal and to have a broad vision, as he/she has to tackle problems not only at the micro- but also macro-level: to be a social transformation actor being able (competent) to understand the complicated social processes and influence these processes, to preserve and inherit cultural and national traditions, to ensure a high quality of communication, interconnections, citizenship, and leisure, and to maintain good health. The focus is placed on a competent individual as the most important precondition for competitiveness; human abilities arethusidentifiedwith humancompetence, as the key goal of human development not only relates to the acquisition of material benefits, but also to the comprehensive development of the individuals' personality. Therefore, the European Commission developed a framework of 8 key competences, including the sense of initiative and entrepreneurship that has to be developed by everyone, beginning from childhood and throughout the entire life. These competences are considered equally important for life and work in a knowledge-based society (European Commission, 2006). Therefore, the concept of entrepreneurial ability may be explained in a much broader – socio-economic – sense than that of entrepreneurial competence. It means that along with professional training, the overall development of an individual as a personality, as well as the development of the individual's key competences, including entrepreneurial competence, has to be ensured.

Entrepreneurial competenceis a set of the individual's personal talents, traits, and abilities. It includes: abilities to create and innovate, communication ability, organisational ability, project management ability, abilities to plan one's own activity and take risk, entrepreneurial ability, as well knowledge and skills needed to establish a new enterprise and embody practical ideas in its successful development. In a broader sense, entrepreneurial competence is characterised bythe personal traits that may be classified into four groups: management competence, social competence, personal competence, and enterprising traits. All the elements of entrepreneurial competence and their interactions are shown in Figure 3.

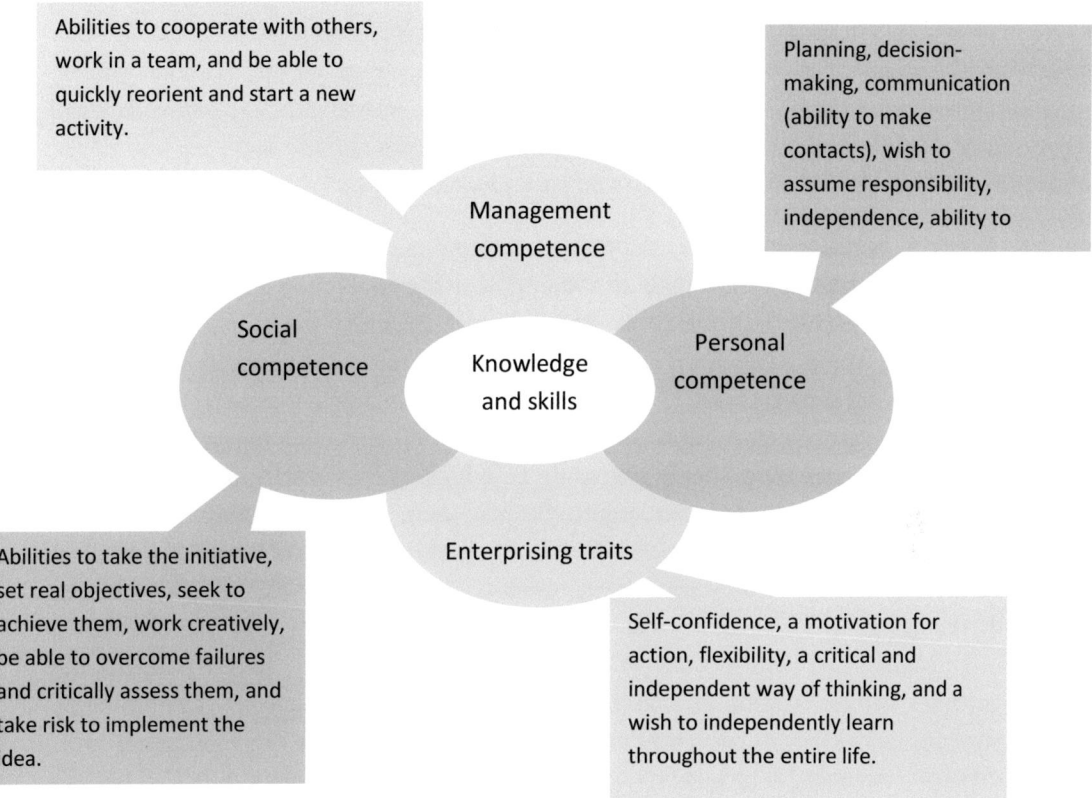

Figure 3.Elements of entrepreneurial competence and their interactions (Bikse, 2011)

Thus, it follows from the qualitative changes in the labour market that nowadays a competent individual, which is given an opportunity to develop his/her entrepreneurial competences along with his/her professional training, is an important precondition of competitiveness.

Challenges in entrepreneurship education in the context of developing entrepreneurial competences

A developed entrepreneurial competence does not yet imply entrepreneurship. It is built through a process of acquiring knowledge, skills, and experience, i.e. an entrepreneurship education process. Entrepreneurship education may be viewed in two senses: *in a broader sense,* it is oriented towards developing a certain set of personal traits and skills, which are important in any field of activity and in life, without directly associating it with establishing new enterprises, while *in a narrow sense,* any particular stage of educational system involves developing specific business skills and acquiring knowledge on how to start up and successfully expand entrepreneurship.

It has to be understood that the task of entrepreneurship education is not only to enable special knowledge and skills in entrepreneurship to be acquired, but the most important is to enable individuals to develop their personal traits and skills (Bikse, Riemere, 2013). This is a much broader perspective on entrepreneurship education than it was until the second half of the 20th century when it was mainly understood as preparing skilful enterprise managers. A.Gibb emphasises that entrepreneurship education has to be viewed much broader than simply preparing individuals as enterprise managers (Gibb, 1999). In this connection, M.Hazans argues that according to the latest studies, such "soft skills" as abilities to work in a team, cooperate, plan and organise, and learn and a creative approach to problems to a greater extent determine the success of individuals in the labour market than "hard skills" when an individual can do something specific (Lulle, 2013). It means that the process of studies has to be oriented towards developing competences and integrating the elements of entrepreneurship education into all study programmes in order to develop entrepreneurial competences in interaction with professional education, which would assist youth to be creative and act in a socially responsible way and would encourage them to choose entrepreneurship or self-employment as a career option (Kirby, 2006; Chiru, Tachiciu, &Ciuchete, 2012).

The concept of entrepreneurship education is very often understood in a too narrow sense – as business activities and as studying only economic courses. Not only those who plan to connect their professional life with economics and management but everyone – future engineers, biologists, physicists, chemists, mathematicians, and others – have to develop their entrepreneurial competences. Therefore, the European Commission documents stress that entrepreneurship education should not be confused with general business and economic studies (European Commission, 2008). Its goal is to promote creativity, innovation, and self-employment (Guidance ..., 2011).

Analysing the modern entrepreneurship education, several authors point out that it still employs the traditional approach, namely, it mainly focuses on teaching the youth, for instance, how to establish a new enterprise in the future (Rasmussen,& Sorheim, 2006).

For this reason, the present educational programmes are very often criticised, as they are designed to target too direct tasks rather than to meet the standards of business environment. They lack the multidimensional aspect of problem solving (Solomon, &Tarabishy, 2005).

The labour market challenges of this, the 21st century, set much higher standards for education – to ensure the preparation of not only knowledgeable and high-qualified professionals, but the most important – to enable the youth to develop themselves as creative and enterprising personalities being ready to take risk, make effective decisions, manage projects, and be personally responsible for everything as well as, when starting their activity, become the self-employed by establishing a micro-enterprise or working remotely. It means that nowadays the content of entrepreneurship education has to be significantly changed and it has to involve not only acquiring theoretical knowledge but also enabling the youth to develop their entrepreneurial competences. Besides, these competences have to be developed from their childhood through implementing various entrepreneurship education programmes at all levels of education system, as well as through lifelong learning.

Entrepreneurship education problems and solutions

In Latvia, some activities are carried out in entrepreneurial education. The activities are offered by *the Ministry of Economics, the State Education Development Agency*, higher schools, and other institutions. Employees, pedagogues, pupils, and students of several Latvia's educational institutions have engaged in various international projects and in cross-border cooperation programmes in the Central Baltic Sea Region. A few elements of entrepreneurial education are integrated in certain school subjects/university courses. At the governmental level, too, a range of activities and initiatives are implemented at all the levels of education system to prepare the new generation for starting up entrepreneurship.

An important instrument promoting entrepreneurship start-ups is the ESF project *"Support for Starting up Self-employment and Entrepreneurship"* implemented by the *Mortgage and Land Bank of Latvia and the Latvian Guarantee Agency*. The project offers consultancy, training, loans, as well as grants for starting up entrepreneurship. Working-age individuals, including the unemployed who wish to start up entrepreneurship as well as entrepreneurs of newly established enterprises and experienced entrepreneurs that intend to produce a brand-new good or service, are eligible for this support. In the project, training is offered in such modules as entrepreneurship basics (small business management), management basics, the legal framework of entrepreneurship, financial management, accounting and taxes for business, and marketing basics. Up to now, 1624 programme participants of various ages have been trained.

Nevertheless, there are problems both in the European Union (EU) and in Latvia that have to be seriously tackled in implementing entrepreneurship education. According to *Global Entrepreneurship Monitoring* studies, Europeans, compared with Americans, are not very eager to take risk, and they are much more reluctant to start up a business. In 2009, 26000 respondents of various ages and demographic groups were questioned, while in 2012, 42000 respondents in all the EU Member States and in 13 non-EU countries were surveyed (Figure 4).

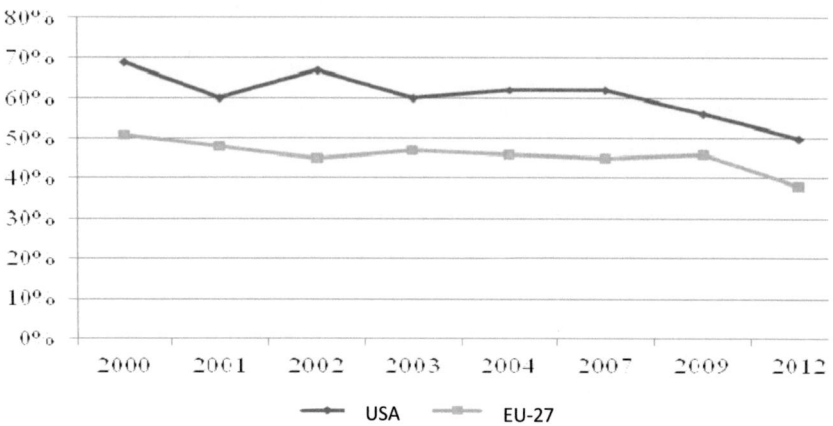

Figure 4.**Choice of the status of self-employed in the USA and EU-15** (as a % of the total number of respondents) (European Commission (EC), 2007; EC, 2009; EC, 2012)

*The period 2000-2007 in the EU-15 (EU Member States before the enlargement in 2004); the period 2009-2012 in the EU-27

As shown in Figure 4, the proportion of those respondents who prefer self-employment has decreased in the USA since 2007 (from 61% in 2007 to 53% in 2012). In contrast, the EU respondents' attitude to self-employment became more positive in 2009, as this study included data on the present EU-27 Member States instead of the EU-15. Yet, according to the latest survey, the proportion of the EU respondents wishing the status of self-employed sharply declined – to only 37% (45% were reported by the previous survey). So this gap between the USA and the EU has not decreased. In Latvia, in contrast, the number of the respondents who wished to become the self-employed was considerably greater (49%) than in the EU-27 (45% in 2009), according to the 2012 survey. However, this proportion, compared with 2007, decreased, as then 50% of the respondents in Latvia wished to obtain the status of self-employed.

The key advantages motivating the majority of the respondents questioned in the EU Member States to obtain the status of self-employed are a possibility to act independently (62%), a free choice of working hours and the place of a job (30%), and a possibility to be independent and fully realise one's potential through doing the work one is interested in. In contrast, the respondents preferring to work as employees consider social protection – not loosing a job and earning a constant and regular income – as the most important advantage. On a question, "Do you have a possibility to become a self-employed person in the next five years?", only 10% of the respondents in the EU-27 gave an answer "*very possible*"; in the USA it was 44 percent. In Latvia, this rate was the highest – 51%.

A survey of pupils in Latvia conducted within the international project "Promotion of Entrepreneurial Skills in Education in Latvia, Estonia, Sweden, and Finland" evidenced that the wish of pupils to found their own enterprise in the future was quite great. Of the pupils in 2011, 66.5% *often* and *always* thought of establishing their own enterprise in the future, while in 2009, 71.2% of the total number of pupils gave such a reply (Bikse, 2011).

This is a positive trend that meets the challenges of the new era. It means that these positive trends have to be taken into consideration in entrepreneurial education. It is important to strengthen these trends by creating a possibility to acquire knowledge and skills and to develop the abilities needed for turning ideas into real activities. It is important not only to teach individuals but also to strengthen their confidence in their abilities, to build up their confidence so that they are able to realise their idea, establish their enterprise, and successfully manage it, consequently dedicating their future career to entrepreneurship. If the youth believe that they possess the needed skills, they will be confident in their abilities, which will encourage them to make all their efforts to achieve their goal. Thus, the greater will be their confidence in the possibilities to establish their own enterprise, the stronger will be their motivation to achieve the desired goal. Yet, according to several surveys, entrepreneurial skills are insufficiently developed in pupils and students. Of the surveyed pupils, only 17.3% in 2011 and 19.7% in 2009 were engaged in establishing and managing pupil enterprises (Bikse, 2011). University graduates rated their skills for starting up entrepreneurship lowest than other skills that build their entrepreneurial competences (Table 3).

Table 3. **Respondents' rating of to what extent they had a possibility to acquire skills building their entrepreneurial competence when studying at a university (%)**

Educational fields	No skill was acquired	Low or very low	Medium	High or very high	No reply
Finding creative solutions to various complicated problems	1.7	13.2	40.4	43.4	1.2
Working with information: its assessment, analysis, and systematisation	4.0	5.1	30.8	62.6	1.1
Working in a team	1.8	10.3	32.6	54.1	1.2
Planning, organising, and	3.5	8.4	33.0	53.7	1.4

managing one's work					
Making decisions based on an analysis of information	1.1	8.7	36.4	52.4	1.4
Presenting information publicly	1.4	11.6	34. %	51.2	1.1
Discussing publicly and justifying one's opinion	2.1	15.1	37.0	44.6	1.2
Working with specific computer applications for an industry	13.1	24.0	34.7	27.0	15.5
Entrepreneurial skills	27.3	31.5	27.1	12.7	1.4

Source: Author's table, according UILE, 2012

Table 3 shows that of the 4909 respondents, 27.3% did not develop entrepreneurial skills at all; 31.5% of the alumni rated their acquired skills as very low and low, while 27.1% assessed their skills as medium. Only 12.7% of the alumni developed their skills needed for starting up entrepreneurship to a high and very high level. A comparison of the survey findings with the respondents' ratings in the educational field *management sciences and administration* shows that they are insufficiently prepared in entrepreneurial education issues. Even though a study programme in management enables students to study almost all courses contributing to developing entrepreneurial competences, yet 30.8% of the respondents pointed out that they had *no possibility to acquire skills for starting up entrepreneurship at all* or they developed such skills to a very low and low level. A large number of the respondents (43.2 %) said that they developed these skills to a *medium level*. It evidences: the European Commission's objectives aimed at developing entrepreneurial competences in all young people by integrating the elements of entrepreneurial education in various higher education programmes and courses, especially in the study programmes of natural sciences and engineering in Latvia's universities, are not fully sought to be achieved even in the study programmes of economics (European Commission, 2008). Not all the universities fully comply with the Cabinet Regulation of the Republic of Latvia

(2001). *"Regulations regarding the National Standard of First as well as Second Level Professional Higher Education"*; the regulation stipulates that study modules of at least six credit points in size have to be integrated in all study programmes (in higher schools – in undergraduate programmes if the programmes had no elements of entrepreneurial education).

Nowadays, a significant challenge of the educational system both in Latvia and in other European countries is to create preconditions so that the youth themselves are able and interested in creating jobs and becoming employers. However, according to the studies, Latvia's educational system mainly focuses on preparing high-qualified professionals as employees in a certain field rather than developing entrepreneurial competences, too, in individuals along with educating them in a certain speciality, so that young individuals are ready to start their business, becoming employers. According to survey only 5% ff the respondents were employers (entrepreneurs) and 6.1% had gained the status of self-employed, inter alia they became self-employed after graduating from university or started their own entrepreneurship. Only 14.4% planned to found a new enterprise, purchase an existing one, or become a self-employed individual during the next three years. The main reasons that prevented the surveyed alumni from starting up entrepreneurship were financial problems (46.2%) and no knowledge and skills needed for establishing their own enterprise (31.8%). Many of them mentioned that entrepreneurship does not guarantee steady income (27.5%) and they were afraid to take risk (27.6%), as well as national administrative procedures were complicated (25.2%) and they had no ideas how to start up entrepreneurship (23.5 %), and the lack of enterprising ability (19.4 %) was also a reason (UILE, 2012).

On an open question, "What higher schools have to do to encourage alumni to engage in entrepreneurship?", the alumni pointed out that it is important to the higher schools "Not to break the backbone of potential entrepreneurs, but to contribute to the creativity of students and their initiatives to implement ideas, give more practical knowledge, offer or simulate the start-up of a business". "Surelyeveryone hastheir own ideaor hobbythatlikes to do; then the universities canhelpto work withthese ideas, develop them, and recommendhow to act, what to give up orhow to taketheir ideato the nextstep tocreate a business out of this idea". "In general, Ithink theuniversity'smission is toinspire,but, unfortunately,more often it involvessome kind of hindrance andcriticism".

To encourage the alumni to engage in entrepreneurship, a university's mission is to ensure the integrity of theory and practice in the study process, enabling students to learn by doing and to demonstratetheir skills ina particularactivity through searching an innovative approach to tackling economic problems. Another important precondition is the creation of an environment contributing to creative thinking, which would promote the generation of new ideas that fascinate, make individuals act, and shape their lifestyle. According to the survey by the Global Entrepreneurship Monitor, 87% of the respondents in the EU-27 pointed to it (European Commission, 2012). Doing what one is fond of and meets one's interests and goal in life is also a success. An importantfactor is to encourage theyoung individualto continue what was started, regardless of any difficulties, to achievethe intended resultsand gainsatisfaction, toidentifypossibilities for turning ideas intorealproducts, and to make every student understand that implementing an idea is adistantgoal–buildingone's own company in the future.

A study programme "Innovative Entrepreneurship" that is successfully implemented by, for instance, the School of Business and Finance could serve for this purpose in higher schools. The authors believe that in this study programme, *establishing student enterprises could be made a mandatory requirement for the entire four-year period of studies* (every student has to be engaged in at least one such a project), so that students go through all the processes of establishing an enterprise – from the very beginning to the moment of production of goods and services – in order to gain a real insight into the foundation and operation of an enterprise. Turība University has started implementing a study approach based on practical education. The future professionals who study in the professional undergraduate programme *Enterprise Management* are offered practical studies in a business incubator where they, along with acquiring knowledge on entrepreneurship, also implement their business ideas by founding enterprises. The university provides premises and a mentor's advice – all the necessary for founding and managing an enterprise. At least four students create an enterprise. During this activity, theychange their rolesso that eachcouldlearnmanagement, marketing, finance and accountancy,and other entrepreneurial skills. For successful entrepreneurship, along with practical activities, students hold meetings with experienced entrepreneurs, attend lectures, independently study special literatures, learn to process information – to assess, analyse, and systemise it and to find creative solutions in order to enhance the services offered by their enterprise and to ensure the expansion of it. Thus, students develop their skills and gain experience in working in a team, jointly plan, hold, and manage their work, learn to "cooperate, agree, make compromises, and jointly make decisions, as the real life shows that in many cases, an enterprise is liquidated because its owners have no mutual consensus", according to

171

A.Rostovskis, chairman of the Development Council of Turība University (Nestere, 2013).

The mentioned examples, as well as the findings of other authors (O'Connor, 2013) evidence that in universities, the study process may be designed in a way that along with acquiring knowledge, students can develop their unique abilities by using the possibility to work practically during the entire period of their studies, which allows them to express themselves in a creative way, independently make decisions and draw conclusions, develop their ability to take responsibility and the initiative and not to be afraid of the unknown, and build confidence in achieving what was intended. It means: in order that the youth could live and work according to the challenges of the 21st century labour market, a new vision on designing higher education programmes is needed. Such an urgent vision requires a complex approach to tackling organisational problems of the study process, focusing mainly on forming personalities and creating opportunities for their self-realisation, so that in the future anyone is able to start up entrepreneurship and create a job for themselves and, what is even better, for others.

Conclusions

According to the labour market forecast, the demand for high-qualified employees will considerably increase in Latvia. The roles of remote working and micro-enterprises in economic growth and the employment of the population will increase. Under such circumstances, the role of individuals in the economy will significantly change: they will become employers to themselves and, at the same time, entrepreneurs and the self-employed. Therefore, the education system has to adapt to the labour market challenges, enabling every young individual to build up their entrepreneurial competences in the process of entrepreneurial education, so that they are prepared to found their own enterprise in the future.

Studies show that the traditional approach to entrepreneurship education is still employed. It is still considered that the task of entrepreneurship education is to teach mainly economic courses rather than to focus on a broader sense – to contribute to the development of a certain set of personal traits. For this reason, while studying at a higher school, almost a third of the respondents had no possibility to acquire skills for starting up entrepreneurship and another third developed their skills to a very low or low level. Therefore, only a small number of university alumni have become employers and obtained the status of self-employed. The majority of them have no special desire to start up entrepreneurship in future, as they lack ideas and enterprising ability, are afraid to take risk, and lack the knowledge and skills needed to establish their own enterprise. It means that our educational system insufficiently focuses on developing entrepreneurial competences in our youth, so that they are prepared to establish their own enterprises in the future.

To prepare competitive and enterprising professionals according to the labour market challenges and to shape the new generation's understanding of entrepreneurship and its desire to engage in it, the task of higher schools in their study process is to balance theory and practice and employ modern teaching methods, giving a greater possibility to students to work practically. In cooperation with entrepreneurs, both professional and academic programmes should be enhanced to include student practical works as orders from private firms or government institutions, based on the needs in the national economy, so that the learning outcomes and good ideas are not wasted. Professionals (guest lecturers) from various fields should be more often invited to lectures and seminars, and students have to be offered a possibility to study interdisciplinary programmes so that the knowledge and skills acquired could be used in tackling intersectoral problems.

It is important to the universities to ensure that courses are delivered by the lecturers who are high-qualified, creative, progressively-minded, and well aware of theories and practices (experienced in practice and research) and who are interested in integrating the elements of entrepreneurial education in their courses. The mission of university lecturers is to assist every student in comprehending and developing their personal traits and abilities, to encourage them to start up entrepreneurship, to promote the generation of ideas and enable students to creatively express themselves (through working independently), to make students confident in success, and to motivate, inspire, and interest them in implementing their creative ideas.

List of References

1. Bikse, V. *Entrepreneurial Abilities.* Riga: Art & Design SIA (2011).

2. Bikse, V., & Riemere, I. *The Development of Entrepreneurial Competences for Students of Mathematics and the Science Subjects: the Latvian Experience.*Procedia - Social and Behavioral Sciences (2013, Vol. 82, p. 511 – 519).

3. Cantillon, R. *An Essay on Economic Theory.* An English translation translated by Saucier C., ed. Thorton M. Auburn, Ludvig Von Mises Institute (2010).

4. Chiru, C., Tachiciu, L., &Ciuchete, S.G. *Psychological factors, behavioural variables and acquired competencies in entrepreneurship education.*Procedia - Social and Behavioral Sciences (2012, Vol. 46, p. 4010 – 4015).

5. European Commission (2012). *Rethinking Education: Investing in Skills for Better Socio-Economic Outcomes.*Strasbourg: COM (2012) 669. Available at: http://ec.europa.eu/education/news/rethinking/com669_en.pdf.

6. European Commission. *Entrepreneurship Education at School in Europe National Strategies, Curricula and Learning Outcomes* (2012). Available at: http://eacea.ec.europa.eu/education/eurydice/documents/thematic_reports/135EN.pdf

7. European Commission. *Effects and impact of entrepreneurship programmes in higher education* (2012). Available at: http://ec.europa.eu/education/news/rethinking/com669_en.pdf.

8. Ministry of Economicsof the Republic of Latvia. (2012). *The forecasts of the medium-term and long-termlabour market in Latvia* (2012). Available at: http://www.em.gov.lv

9. European Commission.*Entrepreneurship in higher education, especially in non-business studies* (2008). Available at: http://ec.europa.eu/enterprise/entrepreneurship/support_measures/training_education/entr_highed.pdf

10. European Commission.*Entrepreneurship education in Europe:Fostering entrepreneurial mindsets through education and learning.* Final Proceedings (2006). Available at: http://ec.europa.eu/enterprise/entrepreneurship/support_measures/training_education/index.htm

11. European Commission. *Final report of the expert group "Best procedure" project on education and training for entrepreneurship* (2002). Available at: http://europa.eu.int/comm/enterprise/entrepreneurship/support_measures/training_education/index.htm

12. European Commission. *Entrepreneurship in the EU and beyond.* Flash Eurobarometer Reports (2007; 2009; 2012). Available at: http://ec.europa.eu/enterprise/public-opinion/flash/fl-en.pdf

13. Gibb, A. *Can we build effective entrepreneurship through management development?* Journal of General Management (1999), Vol. 24, No.4, p. 1 –21.

14. *Guidance supporting Europe's aspiring entrepreneurs.* Policy and practice to harness future potential. Research paper. No 14. Luxembourg: Publications Office of the European Union (2011). Available at: http://www.cedefop.europa.eu/EN/Files/5514_en.pdf.

15. Kirby, D. *Entrepreneurship education: can business schools meet the challenge?* International Entrepreneurship Education. Ed by Fayolle A., Klandt H., UK Edward Elgar Publishing, pp. 35-54 (2006).

16. Lebusa, M. J. *Does Entrepreneurial Education Enhance Under-graduate Students' Entrepreneurial Self-Efficacy?* A Case at one University of Technology in South Africa. China-USA Business Rewiev (2011,Vol. 10, No. 1. p.53–64).

17. Lulle, B. *Demogrāfijas pasākumi ir pareizi, bet izceļošanu nemazina.* NRA, 20.03.2013.

18. Cabinet of Ministers of the Republic of Latvia. Regulations on State Standard on the Second Level Professional Higher Education; Regulations No 481 of 20 November 2001. Available at: http://www.mk.gov.lv/likumi

19. Project of Universities Investment in Latvian Economy (UILE) (2012).Available at: http://www.lu.lv/fileadmin/user_upload/lu_portal/par/strukturvienibas-un-infrastruktura/saist/lua/Universitasu_ieguldijums_Latvijas_tautsaimnieciba.pdf

20. Maršal, A. *Principles of economics:*an introductory vol., New Yourk, The Macmillan Company, fifth printing (1953).

21. McCoonnell, C. R., &Brue, S. L. *Economics: Principles, Problems and Policies.* McGraw-Hill. Irwin (1999).

22. Misra, S., &Kumar, E. S. *Resourcefulness: A Proximal Conceptualisation of Entrepreneurial Behavior.* Journal of Entrepreneurship(2000, Vol. 9, p. 135-154).

23. Nestere, L. *Lai negatavotu bezdarbniekus, jāpiedāvā jauni izglītības risinājumi.* NRA, 05.03.2013.

24. O'Connor, A. *A conceptual framework for entrepreneurship education policy: Meeting government and economic purposes.* Journal of Business Venturing (2013, Vol. 28, p. 546–563).

25. Rasmussen, E.A., & Sorheim, R. *Action-based entrepreneurship education.* Technovation, (2006,Vol. 26, p. 185–194).

26. Say, J.B. *A Treatise on Political Economy; or the Production, Distribution, and Consumption of Wealth,* ed. Clement C. Biddle, trans. C. R. Prinsep Philadelphia: Lippincott, Grambo & Co. (1880).
27. Schumpeter, J.A. *The Theory of Economic Development.* USA, New Brunsvic, Trasaction Publishers (1983).
28. Solomon, G., &Tarabishy, A. *Entrepreneurship Education in the United States: A Preliminary Report.* Proceedings: 15th Internationalizing Entrepreneurship Education and Training (IntEnt) Conference, Guilford, UK (2005).

Publications of the Baltic Sea Academy

Volume 1
Strategies for the Development of Crafts and SMEs
in the Baltic Sea Region
2011
ISBN: 9783842326125

Volume 2
Strategy Programme for education policies in the Baltic Sea Region
2012 (2nd edition)
ISBN: 9783848252534

Volume 3
Education Policy Strategies today and tomorrow around the "Mare Balticum"
2011
IBSN: 9783842374218

Volume 4
Energy Efficiency and Climate Protection around the
Mare Balticum
2011
ISBN: 9783844800982

Volume 5
SME relevant sectors in the BSR: Personnel organisation, Energy and
Construction
2012
ISBN: 9783848202577

Volume 6

Strategies and Promotion of Innovation in Regional Policies around the Mare Balticum

2012

IBSN 9783848218295

Volume 7

Strategy Programme for innovation in regional policies in the Baltic Sea Region

2012

ISBN: 9783848230471

Volume 8

Humanivity - Innovative economic development through human growth by Kenneth Daun

2012

ISBN: 9783848253395

Volume 9

Economic Perspectives, Qualification and Labour Market Integration of Women in the Baltic Sea Region

2013

ISBN: 9783732243952

Volume 10

Corporate Social Responsebility and Women's Entrepreneurship around the Mare Balticum

2013

ISBN: 9783732278459

Volume 11
Development of the enterprises' competitiveness in the context of demographic challenges
2013
ISBN: 973732293971

Volume 12
Age, Gender and Innovation –

Strategy program and action plans for the Baltic Sea Region
2014
ISBN: 9783735784919

Volume 13
Innovative SMEs by Gender and Age around the Mare Balticum
2014
ISBN: 9783735791191

Volume 14
Innovation in SMEs, previous projects in the Baltic Sea Region and future needs
2014
ISBN: 9783735791191

Volume 15
Building the socially responsible employment policy in the Baltic Sea Region
2014
ISBN: 9783735790484

Members of the Hanse-Parlament

The Chamber of Craftmanship and Enterprise in Białystok

Brest Department of the Belarusian Chamber of Commerce and Industry

Hungarian Association of Craftsmen Corporations

Företagarna Kalmar länCottbus Chamber of Skilled Crafts and SME's

Dresden Chamber of Skilled Crafts and Small Businesses

Pomeranian Chamber of Handicrafts for SME's

Hamburg Chamber of Skilled Crafts and Small Businesses

The Federation of Finnish Enterprises

Chamber of Craft Region Kaliningrad

Kaliningrad Regional Economic Development Agency

Chamber of Crafts and SME in Katowice

Chamber of Crafts and SME in Kielce

Handicraft Chamber of Ukraine

Handicraft Chamber Leningrad Region

The Craft Chamber of Łódź

Företagarna Skåne Service AB

Belarusian Chamber of Commerce and Industry

Minsk Department of the Belarussian Chamber of Commerce and Industry

Mogilev Branch of Belarusian Chamber of Commerce and Industry

Russian Chamber of Crafts

Warmia and Mazury Chamber of Crafts and Small Business in Olsztyn

Chamber of Crafts in Opole

The Norwegian Federation of Craft Enterprises

Master of Crafts Norway

Eastern Mecklenburg-Western Pomerania Chamber of Handicraft

Panevėžys Chamber of Commerce, Industry and Crafts

Satakunnan Yrittajät R.Y.

Wielkopolska Craft Chamber in Poznań

Latvian Chamber of Crafts

Craft Chamber in Rzeszów

Schwerin Chamber of Skilled Crafts

The Chamber of Handicraft Middle Pomerania in Słupsk
The St. Petersburg Crafts Chamber
The Chamber of Crafts and SME in Szczecin
Estonian Association of Small and Medium Enterprises
The Baltic Institute of Finland
The Organisation of Handicraft Businesses in Trondheim
Vilnius Chamber of Commerce, Industry and Crafts
Lithuanian Business Employers Confederation
The Chamber of Crafts of Mazovia, Kurpie and Podlasie Regions in Warsaw
Small Business Chamber Warsaw
The Lower Silesian Chamber of Craft and Small and Medium-sized Businesses
Kyiv Chamber of Commerce and Industry
IBC Innovationsfabrikken Kolding
Donskaya Craft Chamber in Rostov/Don
Nordic Forum of Crafts

Members of the Baltic Sea Academy

Brest State Technical University, Belarus
University 21 non-profit limited Liability Company, Germany
Hamburg University of Corporate Education, Germany
Hamburg Institute of International Economics, Germany
Hanse-Parlament e.V., Germany
International Business Academy, Denmark
Lund University, Sweden
Satakunta University of Applied Sciences, Finland
University of Latvia, Latvia
Gdansk University of Technology, Poland
Panevėžys College
Hanseatic Academy of Management, Słupsk, Poland
Saint-Petersburg State University of Economics, Russia
Tampere University of Technology, Finland
Vilnius Gediminas Technical University, Lithuania
Vilnius Pedagogical University, Lithuania
University of Bialystok, Poland
Võru County Vacational Training Centre, Estonia